DATE			

TENURE

by

Bill Wine

PLAYERS PRESS, Inc.
P.O. Box 1132
Studio City, CA 91614-0132

TENURE

© Copyright, 1993, by Bill Wine
and PLAYERS PRESS, Inc.
ISBN 0-88734-263-9
Library of Congress Catalog Number: 93-6131

Library of Congress Cataloging-in-Publication Data

Wine, Bill, 1944-
    Tenure / Bill Wine.
        p.   cm.
    ISBN 0-88734-263-9
    1. Man-woman relationships--United States--Drama. 2. College
teachers--Tenure--Drama.   I. Title.
PS3573.I524T46   1993
812'.54--dc20
                                                    93-6131
                                                      CIP

CAST

Aaron Kaplan

Lydia Sweet

Joel Ginsberg

*(*The following pairs of characters are portrayed by the same actors.*)*
Ned Underwood
Mort Kaplan

George Sullivan
Jeffrey Kaplan

Clara Taylor-Rush
Ronnie Kaplan

Rick Primiano
Terry Sweet

Paul McCarthy
Donald Sweet

Marilyn Carswell
Pat Hightower

*The actors portraying two characters make casual changes – donning outer clothing, removing eyeglasses, affecting different accents – to accommodate their on-stage moves from one character to the other.

SCENE: The action takes place over several years in the 1980's on and near the campus of Union State University, a medium-size college in the northeast United States.

SETTING: A single setting provides the various locales.

The primary set of Act One is that of a conference room. There is a large, rectangular table in the center of the room, upon which have been placed several piles of large, overstuffed notebooks, a stack of filled file folders, a small pile of notepads, several ashtrays, and a water pitcher and drinking glasses. Around the perimeter of the room are additional chairs, two small sofas, a bookcase, a portable blackboard, and a small table or cart holding a coffee urn, cups, and related paraphernalia.

This same set, with some modification of furnishings and props, will suffice as the judge's chambers in Act Two.

During both acts, the D.L. area -- utilized for flashbacks, reminiscences and alternate locales -- will be brightly but separately lit and sparsely furnished as needed (a chair, a couch, a desk, etc.). The D.R. area, utilized for scenes between Aaron and Lydia, will itself be separately lit, in high-contrast cameo, and will also be furnished as sparsely as possible, if at all.

TENURE

ACT ONE

(The conference room, empty of people, has obviously been prepared for an imminent meeting. Paul McCarthy rushes in with an armful of notebooks, which he places on the large table in the middle of the room. He then busies himself with divvying up supplies—ashtrays, pads, pencils, etc.—and making sure everything is in order. Ned Underwood enters, a pair of file folders under his arm.)

NED. Are we all set, Paul?

PAUL. All set, Ned. *(Glances at his watch.)* Right on time.

NED. Plenty of coffee, I hope?

PAUL. Should be. *(Goes to coffee urn to check.)* Yep. Gladys just made it. *(Tugs at his collar.)* Although it's very warm in this room.

NED. As always. *(To Paul as Rick Primiano enters.)* Well, we can send for soft drinks later.

RICK. I thought we were meeting in 216.

NED. Hello, Rick. No, there's a senior seminar in there tonight.

RICK. Not till seven, I thought.

NED. Right.

RICK. We won't be done by seven?

(Ned and Paul laugh.)

PAUL. You must be kidding. Last year we—. This is your first, isn't it?

RICK. Yeah. I guess I shouldn't have made dinner plans, huh?

5

(Marilyn Carswell and Clara Taylor-Rush enter, chatting with each other.)

MARILYN. Look at it this way. It could be worse. You could be reading blue books tonight.

CLARA. Oh, God, please.

MARILYN. Ned, George had to stop at his office. He said he'd be right down, though.

NED. Thanks, Marilyn. *(Looks around.)* Well, why don't we get right to it? *(They all take seats around the table. After a pause, as others settle in.)* I thought I'd just go over the—

(George Sullivan enters and goes directly to a chair.)

GEORGE. *(As he sits.)* Sorry, folks. I had to stop upstairs for a shot of sodium pentathol. *(Others laugh.)* My word, Clara. So glum? We haven't even begun yet.

(Clara smiles unconvincingly.)

NED. Before we start, let me just, um, make a few introductory remarks here—I know most of you have been through this before. But just for the record. The department board you've been elected to is mandated to make a departmental judgement of two of our colleagues in the Communication Department, both of whom are now eligible for tenure. Lydia Sweet is an associate professor in the cinema program. Aaron Kaplan is also an associate professor, in the writing program. Neither of them has been at the associate professor rank long enough to be eligible for promotion to full professor. That's two years away for Lydia, three for Aaron. You've all had a chance to review the full dossiers of both candidates, I trust? *(Affirmative nods all around.)* Good. Uh, the procedure here at Union State is an initial recommendation by the departmental board which then goes to a committee consisting of the deans, the provost, and me, following which it is taken up by the university-wide Tenure and Promotion Committee. *(Opening a file in front of him.)* Tenure, according to the Union State manual, means... *(Searching for the passage.)*

GEORGE. For better or for worse, in sick days and in health, till retirement us do part.

NED. *(Having found it and good-naturedly acknowledged George's joke, he reads.)* "... the confident expectation of holding one's full-time position until retirement for age or permanent disability or separation for adequate cause under due process or because of a financial emergency befalling Union State University." *(Closes folder.)* Anyway. A few reminders. Our policy in the past has been to insist on the confidentiality of these proceedings. That way I can

6

urge you to be candid. Of course, at the same time I want to warn you against getting unnecessarily personal. As for me, because I'm required to carry our judgement and vote to the Deans' Committee, I usually refrain from joining in the discussion. But I will vote. So.

RICK. *(Raises his hand.)* Question, Ned.

NED. Yes, Rick.

RICK. May I ask just how much weight our particular decision carries?

NED. Well, there's no concrete formula. But it's certainly a major factor in both the Deans' Committee decision and the Tenure and Promotion Committee decision. *(Paul raises his hand.)* Paul.

PAUL. In answer to Rick, I think it would be fair to say that a negative vote on our part carries a great deal more weight than a positive one.

MARILYN. Think of it as a letter of recommendation, Rick. If we endorse the candidate, they say, 'Yes, of course: his or her colleagues.' But if we vote no, it's usually curtains. And that means looking for employment elsewhere the following year.

GEORGE. Or, as it's known throughout academe, Boff the Prof.

NED. *(A mild rebuke.)* George.

GEORGE. Sorry.

NED. As always, we will discuss and vote on each candidate independently of any other. With multiple candidates, we have traditionally taken them in alphabetical order. So, unless anyone has an objection, we'll begin with Aaron Kaplan. The floor is open for discussion. *(Silence all around.)* While you get your thoughts in order, let me explain that, in putting himself up for tenure after only four years at Union State, rather than the customary six, Aaron is exercising his right to convert prior experience at another college into two years toward the tenure time requirement.

PAUL. Which will probably hurt his chances.

NED. Right.

RICK. Why?

PAUL. Well, perhaps not here, in the department, where we're all fairly well-acquainted with him. But the members of the university-wide committee could certainly have used the two extra years to get to know him—or at least know of him. To say nothing of the deans.

NED. I quite agree, Paul. In fact, I advised Aaron to wait the full six years. But he was impatient. *(Good-naturedly.)* I think we're all well-acquainted with the energy level at which Aaron operates. So, predictably, he didn't listen when I asked him what I ask everybody in that situation: What's the rush?

(The lights on the conference room fade down as those on the D.L. area fade up. Aaron Kaplan paces back and forth behind an upholstered chair. The actor playing Ned Underwood exits the conference room area and sits

7

down in the upholstered chair as Mort Kaplan, Aaron's father. He is smoking a pipe.)

MORT. What's the rush, Aaron?

AARON. I heard you the first time, Pop.

MORT. Not an easy one to answer, is it?

AARON. None of your questions are easy. You give new meaning to the phrase, 'pop quiz.' I feel like I'm eight years old here.

MORT. Maybe you're acting like it?

AARON. *(Irritated.)* Pop. What is this?

MORT. You tell me.

AARON. The marriage isn't working, so we're splitting up. It's that simple.

MORT. It's never that simple. Is it mutual?

AARON. Sort of.

MORT. *(Derisively.)* Ha! 'Sort of.' Is there another woman?

AARON. No.

MORT. Liar.

AARON. No.

MORT. Liar.

AARON. *(Loudly insistent.)* No!

MORT. Okay, okay. But I still think you're jumping the gun.

AARON. You'd always think that. No matter how long I waited.

MORT. We waited, you mean. This is mutual, remember?

AARON. Look, Pop. I'm not saying this isn't mostly my thing. But I can't wait around for Ronnie to make a move. I know you're fond of her. But it's inevitable. Believe me.

MORT. But you two haven't even had kids yet.

AARON. All the more reason.

MORT. Yeah, but if you had kids, you wouldn't be splitting up.

AARON. Probably true. But we don't.

MORT. Why haven't you?

AARON. I guess we weren't sure enough of the marriage. I sure wasn't. I'd like to someday.

MORT. Y'mean I actually have a shot at grandchildren before the turn of the century?

AARON. You never know. But I can tell you one thing: the ending of this marriage isn't gonna make your chances any worse.

MORT. Can't be worse than waiting for your brother to bring a kid into this world, that's for sure.

AARON. You spoke to Jeff?

8

MORT. Tuesday he called.

AARON. How is he?

MORT. Fine, fine. Stop changing the subject. Look, I'm trying to understand you guys...

AARON. I know.

MORT. ...but you're playing by a different set of rules than we did. Your mother and I were in it for the duration. Period. End of story.

AARON. Fine. Great. That was you.

MORT. *(After a beat.)* Do you wanna know what I see? I see you walking out on a great girl. Have you two gone for any...help?

AARON. So someone can help me to discover that I'm miserable? I already know that.

MORT. You're miserable? You're not miserable.

AARON. In my marriage I am.

MORT. Aaron, look at me. *(Aaron comes around and sits down on the arm of chair.)* Really?

AARON. Really.

MORT. I'm sorry. I didn't know. I figured it was something simpler than that. Like your attention span. I know you're a mensch, Aaron. What you do, you do. *(Squeezes Aaron's arm affectionately.)* Can I ask one practical question?

AARON. Shoot.

MORT. What about your career? Won't you be jeopardizing...?

AARON. *(Standing.)* You think there are no divorces in academia?

MORT. What do I know? They might look at you as unstable. It might make your department chairman think twice about giving you, uh...

AARON. Tenure?

MORT. Tenure.

AARON. First of all, he doesn't give it to me. And second, why would it?

MORT. Well, he might see you as the kind of guy who just up and leaves.

AARON. But that would be my privilege. No one could stop me. That's part of what tenure's all about.

MORT. Marriage too, Aaron.

(The lights on the D.L. area fade down as those on the D.R. area fade up. Lydia Sweet stands in place, her head thrown back and both hands cupped over one eye. On the floor at her feet are a textbook and notebook. Aaron Kaplan enters and watches her curiously as he passes by. Lydia feels around her eye gingerly with one hand.)

LYDIA. *(To herself, in whispered but intense frustration.)* Shit!

9

(Aaron stops and approaches her hesitantly, watching with bemused concern.)

AARON. Um, are you okay?

LYDIA. Yeah. One of my lenses just popped out.

AARON. Anything I can do?

LYDIA. Not really. Thanks anyway.

(Aaron moves a step or two away, but remains to watch as Lydia, unaware of his presence, continues trying unsuccessfully to locate the contact lens. Aaron glances about in both directions.)

AARON. No luck, huh?

LYDIA. *(Surprised.)* Oh, you're still here. Nah, I don't know where it is. *(Feels around on her face for it.)* I need a mirror, but I left my bag in the office.

AARON. How about the ladies' room?

LYDIA. Well, actually, I'm afraid to move from this spot.

AARON. Why?

LYDIA. I can tell you don't wear contacts. If it's not on my person and I move from here, I'll never find it. Plus I might step on it.

AARON. *(Glancing at his watch.)* Well, we better do something. There's gonna be a lot of traffic in this corridor in six minutes.

LYDIA. I know. I've got a class.

AARON. Me too. What can I do?

LYDIA. Well, you could check on the floor right in front of me, if you don't mind. *(Aaron moves toward her.)* Just be careful where you step.

AARON. *(Crouching.)* Right. *(He gets down on all fours and checks the floor.)*

LYDIA. I look ridiculous, don't I?

AARON. *(Still on all fours.)* In an endearing sort of way, yeah.

LYDIA. This is very embarrassing.

AARON. Does this happen often?

LYDIA. Not often, no. Occasionally.

AARON. And where do you usually find it?

LYDIA. In my bathroom. Sometimes on the mirror, sometimes in the sink, sometimes on the floor.

AARON. Tricky little devils, aren't they?

LYDIA. Y'know, it might still be in my eye. Or on me somewhere, although for the life of me I can't find it. *(Aaron stands.)* Would you mind?

(Lydia takes her hands from her face and slowly brings her face down to a normal posture, presenting it for Aaron's inspection. Aaron moves very close to her and begins examining the eye to which she points. After a few

10

seconds, she places one hand above and one hand below the eye, and stretches her eyelids in both directions so as to expose as much of the eye as possible.)

AARON. Oh, my God!
LYDIA. What?
AARON. Hey, you've got nice eyes and everything, but that is grotesque.
LYDIA. Sorry. See anything?
AARON. Nothing I could discuss in mixed company.

(Aaron continues inspecting all areas of her face quite carefully and at very close range. Eventually their eyes are directly opposite one another. They both laugh, but neither of them moves.)

LYDIA. My name's Lydia, by the way. Lydia Sweet. I teach film.
AARON. I know. I've seen you around. I'm Aaron Kaplan. I just started teaching writing here. It's nice to meet you, Lydia. You have nice skin for a human being.
LYDIA. You better get to your class, Aaron. I'll be okay.
AARON. *(Stepping back.)* You sure?
LYDIA. Uh huh. Go, go.
AARON. Okay. *(Starts to exit, then stops.)* Oh. *(Comes back to Lydia.)* Here. *(Holds out his hand.)*
LYDIA. *(Holding out her hand.)* What? *(Aaron places something very carefully in her hand. Lydia looks at it. Surprised.)* My lens! Where was it?
AARON. In my hand.
LYDIA. Before that?
AARON. On the floor.
LYDIA. On the floor? But...
AARON. Gotta go. See ya. *(Exits.)*

(Confused, Lydia looks down at the lens in her hand, then off in the direction of Aaron's exit. The lights on the D.R. area fade down as those on the conference room fade up. Conditions around the room—coffee cups on the table, writing on the blackboard, cigarettes in the ashtrays, files and notebooks scattered and opened—indicate that it is some time later at the same meeting. Ned stands at the coffee urn, pouring himself a cup. The others sit around the table as before.)

MARILYN. *(Haphazardly leafing through a notebook.)* What especially strikes me about Aaron's record of publications is its diversity—he's written on a very impressive array of topics. *(She looks around for response.)*

PAUL. In one respect, I agree. As a journalist, he's surely covered more than his share of areas. However, from an academic standpoint, there is very little evidence of his ability—or interest, for that matter—in tackling scholarly writing. And I think that has to be seen as a shortcoming.

RICK. I guess that's true. But Aaron is a journalist, after all. And a teacher of journalism. It seems to me that this is the most appropriate kind of writing for him to be doing.

MARILYN. I have to agree with Rick. We're not a graduate program. If we offered a graduate degree in journalism, I could see the need for faculty to move in the direction of scholarly writing about journalism. But for someone training and turning out undergraduates in journalism, I think Aaron's being a practitioner—and a prolific one at that—is a major plus.

PAUL. Perhaps. But I will still be surprised if it doesn't weigh against him when he comes up for promotion to full professor.

MARILYN. Yes, but that's still several years away. We're here to evaluate Aaron as a candidate for tenure. And I think the nuances of his publication record have less bearing on our tenure recommendation than his service to the university—which we've already determined to be excellent—and his teaching.

NED. May I suggest that we move the discussion in the direction of Aaron's record as a teacher? Any thoughts?

(Rick reaches for one of the notebooks. Clara gets up to get herself a cup of coffee.)

RICK. *(Leafing through the notebook.)* I would say his students see him as someone who works them hard and expects a lot, but who knows his stuff beyond question. Some complaints about his grading being too harsh...

GEORGE. So what else is new?

RICK. *(Agreeing.)* Right.

MARILYN. I think Aaron's expertise and capability shine through on his student evaluations. *(Looking through some notes.)* But there was one thing... I jotted down some notes as I went through these... Here it is. I noticed that a few—no, more than a few; a lot—of Aaron's students either complained or mentioned in passing his... what shall we call it?... his... brutal frankness. Some called it honesty, but even more labeled it meanness or insensitivity. I'm not at all sure how to interpret that.

(Clara returns to her seat at the table.)

PAUL. Apropos of that, quite a few students—women, mostly—commented on his language .

12

RICK. That it was indelicate, you mean?

PAUL. Indelicate, colorful, dirty, salty, obscene, profane. Same difference.

GEORGE. That's hilarious. Getting their sensibilties offended in the classroom during the day so they can feel pure in the evening renting porno movies from the video store.

(George goes to coffee table.)

MARILYN. Well, I think it depends on the extent. I'm assuming, since profanity doesn't seem to be prominent in Aaron's writing, that it's a conscious technique in his teaching. Rather than a lack of discipline or self-restraint.

PAUL. I don't see how it can be a classroom 'technique.' Clara, you teach journalism. What's your view?

CLARA. *(Preoccupied, hesitant to answer.)* Well, it's just Aaron's style, I guess. I'm not sure.

PAUL. I think it is relevant. Since we don't actually monitor teachers in the classroom, these student evaluations are our only source of information about this sort of thing.

GEORGE. *(From coffee table.)* What 'sort of thing'? *(Comes back toward table.)* We're not really going to sit here and discuss his classroom vocabulary, are we? If he chooses to keep his euphemisms to a minimum, and a few overprotected or hypocritical adolescents get their feathers ruffled, well, so be it. Like all of us, Aaron uses whatever language is necessary to get his students off their asses.

PAUL. No one's disputing his effectiveness as a motivator. We're merely discussing tactics.

MARILYN. And tact. There are other ways, George.

GEORGE. There are other ways of doing a lot of things. This is Aaron's way. And it works. All I know is, while I've had my troubles over the years with colleagues' disapproval of things about me that were none of their damn business, I've always appreciated Aaron's combination of straight shooting and open-mindedness. So I want to give him the same leeway he's always afforded me. If he wants to punctuate his lectures with expletives, that's his business. He's a big boy now.

(The lights on the conference room fade down as those on the D.L. area fade up. Aaron, wearing a jacket and tie, sits on a bench, watching things going on across the room. The actor playing George Sullivan exits the conference room area and approaches the bench as Jeffrey Kaplan, Aaron's brother, also dressed semi-formally. Smiling, Aaron slides over to make room. Jeffrey sits down next to him.)

13

JEFF. You're a big boy now. Why can't Aunt Doris dance with you for a change?

AARON. I think she's afraid to, Jeff.

JEFF. How'd you manage that, little brother?

(Both of them watch people on the dance floor in front of them as they speak.)

AARON. I used an old blind-date trick from my fraternity days.

JEFF. *(Intrigued.)* Yeah?

AARON. At Mitchell's Bar Mitzvah, when she pulled me onto the dance floor, I faked a sneezing attack. Gave her one of these. *(Aaron looks right at Jeff and fakes a loud, wet, violent sneeze, from which Jeff recoils.)* I told her I was allergic to her perfume. Which wasn't far from the truth. Then, when I scrunched up my face to do it again, she covered up her face and hair and bolted off the dance floor.

JEFF. *(Laughing.)* I wouldn't bother attending the reading of her will if I were you.

AARON. You can have my share. It'll probably be a year's supply of that perfume.

JEFF. I doubt if I'll be mentioned.

AARON. You? Jeffrey, her twinkle-toes dance partner? Be serious.

JEFF. The dancing is just so she can drop names of young women she wants me to take out. When Mom died, she must have handed off the baton to Aunt Doris. And she never stops trying.

AARON. To turn you around?

JEFF. No. To marry me off.

AARON. *(Surprised, looks at Jeff.)* She doesn't know?

JEFF. Apparently not.

AARON. *(Smiling obligingly as he waves at someone across the room.)* That's impossible. Even if Mom never said anything to her, Pop must have by now.

JEFF. I don't think so. Although I'm sure she... *(With mock pomposity.)* 'has her suspicions.'

AARON. *(Laughing as he looks around the room.)* What about the others?

JEFF. *(Surveying the room.)* Nope. Just Pop. *(Looks at Aaron.)* And you. You've been great, Aaron. Especially with Pop. I want you to know I appreciate it.

AARON. Don't be silly. I love you. *(Surveying the room.)* How do you know everyone else wouldn't react the same way?

JEFF. What are you, kidding? Instant outcast. I don't need that kind of aggravation. I've even perfected my brown-nose laugh at Uncle Nat's faggot jokes. *(Jeff demonstrates a silent, rollicking laugh, slapping his knee and*

14

elbowing Aaron.)

AARON. How do you think Mom would have taken it?

JEFF. *(With a trace of bitterness.)* Who the hell knows? She wouldn't have been so thrilled about you splitting up with Ronnie either. You're not doing this just to take the heat off me, are you?

AARON. Call it an early Channukah gift.

JEFF. Y'know something? *(Looking around the room.)* If everybody here knew I was gay, right now they'd be having their doubts about you too.

AARON. *(Mimicking someone.)* There's something funny about these Kaplan brothers, don't you think?

JEFF. *(Mimicking someone else.)* Nah. You watch. In a couple of years, they'll both be married with kids.

AARON. *(Looking at each other and reciting in unison.)* From your mouth to God's ears. (They laugh.)

(The lights on the D.L. area fade down as those on the D.R. area fade up. Lydia sits at a small table, writing as she eats her lunch. Aaron enters from upstage of her, carrying a cafeteria lunch tray, and leans over her shoulder.)

AARON. Do you really have work to do? Or are you just trying to convince everybody that you enjoy eating alone?

LYDIA. *(Raising her arms in mock surrender.)* It's real. I swear. Deadline at sundown.

AARON. *(Starting to exit.)* I'll let you be then.

LYDIA. *(Turning around.)* No, no, Aaron. It doesn't matter. *(She pushes the work away and makes room for him.)* Sit with me.

AARON. *(As he sits down next to her.)* How are you?

LYDIA. Fine. I read your piece on alimony in the Sunday paper.

AARON. Uh oh.

LYDIA. How's it feel to be on the National Organization of Women's Ten Most Despised list?

AARON. *(Standing and picking up tray.)* Well, nice chatting with you.

LYDIA. *(Taking hold of his arm.)* Sit down. Not to worry. *(Aaron sits.)* Some of my best friends are misogynists.

AARON. Hey. Gimme a break here. That stuff was about certain estranged and deranged wives, not women in general. You obviously took it personally.

LYDIA. Not really.

AARON. Besides, look who's talking. Keep in mind that I read your review of the Clint Eastwood film yesterday. Speaking of diatribes about the opposite sex.

LYDIA. That wasn't a dia... *(They look at each other.)* Truce?

15

AARON. Truce. But I have a question. Just out of curiosity. Why do you use your husband's last name for your byline? Or here, for that matter.

LYDIA. Why? I don't seem the 'type,' you mean?

AARON. No. It just surprises me.

LYDIA. Well, my career got underway before my consciousness got raised, for one thing. And by the time I got a trifle established, I didn't want to confuse the modest following I already had. For another, Lydia Sweet has a lyrical sound to it, don't you think?

AARON. What was your, uh, you should excuse the expression, maiden name?

LYDIA. Luckenbill. Lydia Luckenbill!

AARON. I see what you mean.

LYDIA. Does your wife use your name?

AARON. Yes. Mostly in vain.

LYDIA. *(Sarcastically.)* She must have loved your article. Did she take it personally?

AARON. God, I hope so.

LYDIA. Doesn't your name on a piece like that put a strain on your marriage?

AARON. Believe me, that is spittin' in the ocean.

LYDIA. Your glibness must drive her crazy.

AARON. Why, would it drive you crazy?

LYDIA. I don't know. Maybe.

AARON. What drives you crazy about your husband? *(Lydia doesn't immediately answer.)* Sorry. Forget it.

LYDIA. No, that's okay. Nothing, really. Nothing drives me crazy. We get along great.

AARON. Well, if that's true, whatever you two got, you should bottle it.

LYDIA. *(After a long pause.)* Of course, it helps being separated.

AARON. *(Trying unsuccessfully to contain his surprise, he drops whatever food he's holding and spills the drink.)* Oh. I didn't know.

(Lydia takes a napkin and helps clean Aaron up.)

LYDIA. Nobody here knows. You're the first person I've told.

(They look at one another. The lights on the D.R. area fade as those on the conference room fade up. Conditions indicate that it is a short time later at the same meeting.)

PAUL. What about Aaron's essay? I'm interested in how people responded to that.

RICK. I thought it was really eloquent.

MARILYN. I agree. But even more important, I think it was both heartfelt and realistic. Although it would be helpful to be able to evaluate Aaron's progress and accomplishments in the light of why he was hired in the first place.

PAUL. Right. I think it behooves us to ascertain whether Aaron has performed up to the department's original expectations of him. Has he added to the journalism program the dimension he seemed to offer when he came aboard?

(No immediate response from anybody.)

GEORGE. This isn't exactly something that can be measured quantitatively. It seems rather obvious that Aaron's been a valuable addition, doesn't it?

(Another expectant silence.)

NED. Clara, what about you? Any thoughts?

CLARA. Not really, no.

MARILYN. Clara, forgive me, but... I'm afraid I don't understand your reluctance to share your input with us. I think we more or less expected your insight as a journalism professor and as the person most directly responsible for bringing Aaron to Union State. May I ask? Is it that you feel unfairly biased in his favor?

(Clara looks at Marilyn but says nothing.)

NED. If I may. Just in case that is the reason for your reticence, Clara, I would like to say that I think your feelings and opinions in this regard would be helpful anyway. I hope you can trust us to keep them in perspective.

(Pause.)

RICK. This doesn't seem fair to Clara somehow. I think we should just move on. What about the...

CLARA. *(Emotionally.)* I'm so upset, I don't know what to say.

MARILYN. What is it, Clara? What's the trouble?

CLARA. I'm privy to certain information. It's distressing and maybe it's important, I don't know. But it's also quite personal. And it's about both candidates.

PAUL. Both candidates?

CLARA. Yes. I apologize for my lack of participation today, but this has me discombobulated. I'm just not sure how to handle it.

MARILYN. You mean whether or not to disclose it?

CLARA. I'm just not sure that I have the right. Not that it was something told to me in confidence. On the other hand, sharing it with this committee might very well be my responsibility. I just don't know. *(A long pause. Silence all around. Deliberately.)* Two days ago I found out, quite by accident, that, unbeknownst to all of us in the department, Aaron and Lydia are... virtually living together.

MARILYN. But that's impossible. They have...

CLARA. Take my word for it. It's true.

GEORGE. So what? What does that have to do with anything?

CLARA. I'm not exactly sure, George. But it's at least confusing.

GEORGE. What it is is irrelevant.

PAUL. Now wait a second, George. We were all voted onto this committee by our colleagues. If Clara or anyone here feels something of this nature is pertinent...

GEORGE. *(Bolting out of his seat.)* To say nothing of out-of-order and none-of-our-damn-business.

NED. Easy, George.

GEORGE. *(Standing away from the table.)* This committee has no right to pass judgement on something like this. None whatsoever. It has absolutely no bearing on what we're here to decide, which is whether a faculty member has proved himself, or herself, on the job to a degree that warrants the granting of tenure. Who the hell are we to be discussing a colleague's private life? If I remember correctly, that's what the word private means.

CLARA. *(Standing.)* I understand your feelings, George. But I have to disagree. I think if you'd take some time to think of the long-range implications, you'd realize that we can't ignore this.

GEORGE. Maybe we can't, but I sure as hell can. I'm just as offended by this whole discussion as you apparently are by the after-hours behavior of the candidates. If we don't call a halt to this travesty, I'm leaving.

CLARA. George, please. What do you mean, you're leaving?

(The lights in the conference room fade down as those on the D.L. area fade up. Aaron stands off to one side, quite a distance away from a table and chair. The actress playing Clara exits the conference room area and sits down in the chair at the table as Ronnie Kaplan, Aaron's wife, a liquor bottle and glass in front of her.)

RONNIE. What do you mean, you're leaving? You want a drink?

AARON. No. *(Softly.)* For good, Ronnie. My stuff's already in the car.

RONNIE. Stop this silliness. Sit down. I'll get you something to eat.

18

(Ronnie stands. Aaron turns to exit.) Aaron.

AARON. *(Turning to face her.)* What?

RONNIE. What's going on here? Are we fighting? I don't understand. *(No answer from Aaron. Ronnie sits.)* What'd I do?

AARON. Nothing, nothing.

(Ronnie pours a drink and holds it out to him. Aaron merely looks back at her without moving. She drinks from it herself.)

RONNIE. Tell me what's on your mind.

AARON. Ronnie, I'm going. It's over.

RONNIE. Don't be ridiculous.

AARON. Today it's ridiculous. The last dozen times you suggested it, it was inevitable. Don't worry, by Wednesday it'll be inevitable again.

RONNIE. C'mon, Aaron, we do this all the time.

AARON. No, you do this all the time. When have I ever? *(Ronnie takes a drink.)* This is not an ultimatum, Ronnie. This is real.

RONNIE. I've always come back.

AARON. Exactly.

RONNIE. And so will you.

AARON. We'll see.

RONNIE. Aaron, you've just talked yourself into some crazy notion, that's all. You look so foolish. Let's go to bed. Is that it? *(No answer.)* Aaron. *(Aaron turns to go.)* Aaron, if you go, I won't...

AARON. *(Interrupting.)* You won't what? Take me back? What an idiotic threat that is.

(Ronnie starts to say something, but thinks better of it and stops.)

AARON. Good-bye, Ronnie.

(Aaron exits. Ronnie takes another drink. The lights on the D.L. area fade down as those on the D.R. area fade up. Lydia sits at a desk, working. There is a knock at the door.)

LYDIA. Come in, Aaron.

(Aaron enters.)

AARON. Was it my unmistakable, purposeful stride or just my familiar knock?

LYDIA. Neither. It was that you're the only one coming. Charles can't make the meeting. *(Aaron smiles.)* Try not to look so disappointed. *(Aaron pulls up a chair and sits.)* He had to proctor an exam.

AARON. Should we make it tomorrow?

LYDIA. Can't. With or without Charles, we have to give the Dean our decision by this afternoon.

AARON. Okay, committee chairperson. *(Aaron takes a crumpled sheet of paper out of his pocket.)* I went through the candidates' records last night. I'd say there are only three students who qualify on all counts for the Perry Award. *(He smoothes out the paper and places it in front of her.)* I ranked my choices in descending order.

LYDIA. *(Comparing Aaron's notes to her own.)* I take it the three circled ones are . . . yeah. One . . . two . . . three . . . Well, we have the same three choices, but different ranks. You've got Dennis McMillan first and Sharon Scarborough second, I've got Scarbourough first and McMillan second. Aligning ourselves with the same-sex candidate, predictably. Of course, without Charles, we've got no tie-breaker. So I guess we should forget about the third-place student, whom we agree on, and talk about the relative strengths of the top two. How about if you go through why you voted for McMillan, and then I'll tell you why I picked Scarborough. What do you think?

AARON. *(Sotto voce.)* I think I love you.

LYDIA. *(Who couldn't have heard that correctly, looks at him.)* What?

AARON. I think that's a good idea . . .

LYDIA. *(Turning back to the notes.)* Oh.

AARON. And I think I'm falling in love with you.

LYDIA. *(Flabbergasted.)* Aaron.

AARON. I'm sorry, I'm sorry, I'm sorry, I'm sorry. Forgive me.

(Lydia looks at Aaron for a long moment without speaking.)

LYDIA. Now I know what it feels like to have a tree trunk fall on you.

AARON. Oh, God.

LYDIA. It feels good.

AARON. *(Shocked.)* It does?

LYDIA. Yeah.

AARON. *(After a beat.)* If I don't kiss you soon, I'm gonna need a sedative.

(Lydia moves toward Aaron and they kiss.)

AARON. You win. Give it to Scarborough.

(They laugh and kiss again. The lights on the D.R. area fade down as those on the conference room fade up. It is later at the same meeting. George stands

20

behind his seat at the table, his hands gripping the backrest of the chair. Paul stands at his seat. Clara sits on an upstage sofa. The others sit in their seats.)

PAUL. That is not the point, George.

GEORGE. *(Angrily.)* On the contrary. That is precisely the point.

NED. Ladies and gentleman. *(Stands.)* We must not let our emotions run away from us. Please sit down. *(Paul sits. George sits.)* Clara. *(Clara returns to her seat at the table.)* Thank you. Now. I think it would be a good idea for us to proceed with our discussion, but without losing sight of the absolute need for cool heads and rational behavior to prevail. I know I don't need to remind you that ours is a very important decision—important for the university and important for the two individuals—individuals—whose careers and lives are being scrutinized, discussed, and evaluated today. However, perhaps I should remind you once again of our commitment to keep each candidate separate from and independent of all other candidates and considerations for the duration of the deliberations. We are now fairly well along in our discussion of Aaron Kaplan. Please restrict your comments and questions to Aaron's qualifications as a candidate for tenure. The floor is open. *(Silence.)*

MARILYN. I'm sorry, Ned, but I'm afraid I feel that, under the circumstances, such a restriction is counter-productive. What we want to do here is facilitate communication, not limit it so narrowly.

GEORGE. Marilyn, I disagree. The issue here is not freedom of speech. This is not a casual conversation but a formal procedure. As such, it has boundaries. If we ignore those boundaries, we are doing no less than invading people's privacy.

CLARA. I assure you, I am not trying to invade anyone's privacy. But if I'm to take my responsibility as a voting member of this committee seriously, I have to express my feelings about this matter. The alternative is for me to refrain altogether from participating in the discussion, and then abstain.

GEORGE. Maybe you should.

MARILYN. I can't see what good that would do.

GEORGE. What is the medical proverb? At least do no harm.

CLARA. George, I can't help it. I'm... offended.

GEORGE. Who are you to be offended?

CLARA. These are our colleagues. Do we simply ignore their behaviors, their values?

GEORGE. Some of them, yes. Like the ones that have nothing to do with their performance as teachers and scholars. What does any of this have to do with you?

MARILYN. Now wait a second, George. We're being asked to pass judgement—that's what it is, judgement—on two candidates for permanent residence in this... community.

NED. Ladies and gentlemen, I'm afraid we're lumping the candidates once again. We really must not.

PAUL. Ned, I know our charge is to do otherwise. But it hardly seems possible to keep the candidates entirely separate in this particular instance.

NED. I'm not saying it's easy. I'm saying it's crucial. Rick, you look troubled.

RICK. I guess I'm confused.

NED. About what?

RICK. Well, I'm not sure. (*Looks around.*) Unlike everyone else here, I've never been through this procedure before, either as a candidate or as a committee member. I have no idea whether this discussion is typical or atypical or what. I do know that I feel uncomfortable passing this kind of judgement. Maybe everyone does, I don't know. It's just that I feel, as an untenured, relatively new faculty member at Union State, that I haven't yet earned the right. I was surprised to be elected to this committee in the first place. I assumed it was by default—you know, that I hadn't been around here long enough to amass a gang of political enemies. But now that I'm here, it's difficult to stay as detached as I thought I would. So I'm torn. I'm like everyone else—I have opinions about every issue that's been raised. But every time I volunteer to speak, I feel like the dummy of a ventriloquist who keeps repeating the same line: It's none of my business. It's none of my business.

(The lights on the conference room fade down as those on the D.L. area fade up. Lydia stands behind a couch. The actor playing Rick exits the conference room area and lies down on the couch as Terry Sweet, Lydia's son, a book in his hands.)

TERRY. It's none of my business, Mom.

LYDIA. What's that supposed to mean? I just want your opinion. Look, Terry, I'm not asking for your blessing. Just share your perception with me.

TERRY. My perception is that I want to read now. (*He lifts and opens the book.*)

LYDIA. (*Grabbing the book.*) Terry.

TERRY. This is homework I'm doing, y'know.

LYDIA. I know. Just answer me and I'll let you get back to it.

TERRY. If I did this to you while you were working, you'd scream bloody murder.

LYDIA. One of the privileges of motherhood.

TERRY. (*Sitting up.*) Why does what I think matter, all of a sudden?

LYDIA. What you think always matters. Besides, you have a unique perspective on this relationship.

TERRY. Why's that?

LYDIA. *(Sitting down next to him and handing him his book.)* Because you're the only person at Union State who knows about it.

TERRY. I don't see what the big deal is. Since when aren't professors allowed to date each other? Why are you embarrassed?

LYDIA. I'm not embarrassed.

TERRY. You could've fooled me.

LYDIA. C'mon. Tell me. What was he like?

TERRY. This is stupid. What do you want to hear, that he gave lengthy reading assignments and killer exams? So what?

LYDIA. No. Tell me what he was like in class. Was he funny? Was he mean? Did the girls like him?

TERRY. What are you, twelve years old, all of a sudden? I can't remember.

LYDIA. You can so. It was last semester.

TERRY. Why didn't you ask me this stuff before you went out with him? Why now?

LYDIA. We didn't go 'out,' exactly. It just sort of . . . happened. You know. You seem uncomfortable. Are you...jealous, or anything like that? Is loyalty to your father operating here?

TERRY. Could be. Look, he was okay, I guess. I didn't do so great in his course, but that was my fault, not his. At least he wasn't a goofball or anything. It's just weird to think of him sleeping with my mother.

LYDIA. *(Disapproving.)* Terry.

TERRY. Let's not be childish, Mom, okay? I don't figure on you guys going to the dorm dance and being home by ten. It's okay. I've seen you with men before.

LYDIA. This is different.

TERRY. I know. That's why what I think doesn't matter. Suppose I hated his guts.

LYDIA. That would matter, Terry. It would. But I know you don't.

TERRY. Then stop bugging me. *(Opens the book again.)*

LYDIA. Okay. *(Stands, walks around behind the couch, and watches him read for a moment.)* Terry.

TERRY. *(Lowering the book.)* If I fail this quiz tomorrow, I'm telling Old Man Perkins it was your fault.

LYDIA. This might develop into a serious relationship, Terry.

TERRY. Who are you kidding? It already is.

LYDIA. And?

TERRY. And...I think it's fine.

LYDIA. And?

TERRY. And...you have my qualified permission. Where have I heard that before?

LYDIA. Very funny. And?

TERRY. And...I just can't help wondering where all this guilt is coming from.

LYDIA. What makes you say that?

TERRY. You make me say that.

LYDIA. Terry, please. Translate.

TERRY. Well, the two of you have turned it into this big secret. I figure that means one of two things. Either you feel in your hearts that the relationship is doomed -- in which case you're only asking for trouble. Or you're having such an amazing time that you're expending all your energy keeping those stupid smiles of satisfaction off your faces. *(Lydia stands and turns away.)* Jeez, Mom, I'm sorry.

LYDIA. *(Turning to face him.)* For what?

TERRY. For...I don't know...invading your privacy. *(Beat.)* Wow. I never saw you blush quite that way before.

LYDIA. Terry, stop. Please. I'm sorry I interrupted you. Study.

TERRY. Mom.

LYDIA. Yeah.

TERRY. If you are serious about this guy, you better start thinking about when you're gonna let people know. I think I could adjust to living with somebody else, but not if I was never allowed to tell anybody.

(Terry goes back to his book. Lydia comes around the couch.)

LYDIA. How come a smart kid like you doesn't get better grades?

TERRY. Too many distractions on the home front.

(Lydia kisses him on the head and exits. The lights on the D.L. area fade down as those on the conference room fade up. It is later at the same meeting, during a break. There is a tray of soft drinks on the table. Marilyn and Clara, the only people in the room, sit on the couch, chatting quietly. Ned and Paul enter, pick up drinks, and go to their seats. George enters and goes to the coffee urn. Rick enters and goes to the couch, where he says something quietly to Marilyn and Clara.)

NED. (Looking at his watch.) Shall we re-convene?

(The others move to their seats, some of them picking up drinks along the way.)

GEORGE. *(As he moves toward his seat, having taken a sip of his soft drink.)* This martini has entirely too much ginger ale in it. How's yours, Marilyn?

MARILYN. *(Smiling.)* Scrumptious, George, thanks. I'm feeling light-headed already.

(George and Marilyn raise their drinks in a mock toast gesture and take sips. Everyone sits.)

NED. Well, folks, I thought about your decision during the break and, while I still disagree with it in principle, I don't wish to hold things up. Furthermore, I realize that a five-abstention vote will get us nowhere. So, as you wish, we will dispense with the vote on Aaron Kaplan until after we've discussed both candidates. This is an unprecedented procedure, you realize, one which it will behoove me to mention in my report to the Deans' Committee. But that's what I'll do. So. The floor is open for a discussion of the qualifications of Lydia Sweet.

(A moment of silence, then Clara speaks up.)

CLARA. I'll start, I guess. I would say Lydia's teaching record is solid. Not exemplary, perhaps, but certainly respectable. Judging from the evaluations, her students seem to find her knowledgeable, interesting, and appropriately demanding.

RICK. *(Leafing through one of the notebooks on the table.)* I'll say this. Lydia may not get the highest possible ratings from her students, but hardly any of them give her low grades for any phase of her work. That's pretty impressive, I think.

GEORGE. I'm equally impressed with her apparent openness. Did you notice how many students commented on her encouragement of dissent and criticism? That's a principle we all endorse, sure, but how many of us really implement it as we race through our material? I wish I were as flexible as she seems to be.

CLARA. There is one area that did yield a number of complaints. There were a few criticisms about things like classes missed, papers not graded immediately, and agendas changed at the last minute. These strike me as all traceable to the same source, and that is the demands of Lydia's other professional commitments.

MARILYN. That's true, Clara, but I think it works both ways. It seems to me that for every student who complained, there were four or five who stated that they enjoyed, or even admired, that Lydia practices what she preaches. Her being a practitioner seems to add a valuable dimension in the classroom.

RICK. Let me second that. I can tell from casual conversations with students that they read Lydia's reviews with great interest. And they tell me that her use of her own reviews in class -- and, as George was saying, her willingness to entertain criticism-- makes for stimulating sessions in which students get to see the practical application of theoretical principles.

MARILYN.   Speaking of Lydia's film reviews, I enjoyed reading through a number of them.   She's obviously both an astute critic and a very persuasive writer.   And the impressive scholarly essays she's done for academic journals -- which I can't pretend to fully understand, by the way -- amply demonstrate her expertise.   She seems equally comfortable in both the esoteric and popular arenas.

GEORGE.   Could this be the next Pauline Kael in our midst?

PAUL.   Actually, I'd like to address that very question, George.   Is it advisable for us to be recommending tenure for someone quite so ambitious outside of academe?

RICK.   As a critic, you mean?

(Paul nods.)

MARILYN.   On the other hand, Paul, do we want to punish someone for the sin of achieving too high a degree of success in the pursuit of a completely legitimate professional activity?

PAUL.   A good point.   What I'm asking, I suppose, is whether Lydia's Union State connection is merely a useful and convenient platform from which she is in the process of launching a career which will eventually take her from us?

GEORGE.   There's no guarantee any of us will stay.

RICK.   Besides, Paul, if she were planning on leaving, why would she even want tenure?

NED.   If I may, let me just point out, Rick, that Lydia is automatically up for tenure at this point in her Union State career whether she wants to be or not.

CLARA.   You know, I really don't know how motivated Lydia is about being granted tenure.   Unlike most of our colleagues, she rarely if ever discusses it. And, frankly, her essay sheds very little light on her Union State goals.

GEORGE.   Wait a minute.   We're here to evaluate how well Lydia has performed in three categories — teaching, professional activities, and service to the Union State community.   It's not our function to guess at her or anyone else's ultimate ambitions.

CLARA.   Well, it strikes me that we've seen vivid evidence today of Lydia's disregard for accepted standards of behavior at Union State.   Her surreptitious relationship with Aaron Kaplan is just one example from among a host...

NED.   Clara, Clara.   We're still trying to keep the candidates separate.

CLARA.   Okay, then.   Let's look at her service to the campus community. I for one find it woefully lacking.   And I can't help but interpret that as an indication of Lydia's priorities, among which the Union State community does not seem particularly high.   So I ask two questions: How badly can Lydia want tenure at Union State if she has contributed so little to campus life? And, if her record of service is so thin thus far, why should we expect it to improve later?

GEORGE. How badly Lydia wants tenure is, I repeat, irrelevant.

MARILYN. I'd like to respond to Clara's second question. I think we have to be careful about how we define service to the university. Faculty members who are in the public eye also do service in their own way. Their good work, good name, good deeds—all bring credit to the college, remember, in terms of publicity, prestige, recruitment.

PAUL. Quite true. However, may I try another approach here? As I see it, one of our responsibilities is to pass judgement on the advisability of this university investing -- literally -- in a faculty member for the next several decades. *(Rises and goes to blackboard.)* Now this may seem a crass approach, but bear with me for a minute. *(Erases blackboard, picks up chalk, and writes figures on the board as he speaks.)* In granting tenure to a teacher in, say, his or her thirties, we are committing the university to a commitment of...let's see...let's say, conservatively, an average of...um...forty-thousand dollars a year for perhaps as many as thirty years. That comes to... *(Writes the total on blackboard.)* ...well over a million dollars. It seems to me, then, that if we are to encourage the administration to invest this much money in a human resource, there are two scenarios we want to avoid. One sees a faculty member gaining tenure, working for several years, then moving onto greener pastures -- not such a tragedy financially, to be sure, but forcing us to look elsewhere and, as it were, begin over again. The other sees a person awarded tenure and then proceeding to go through the years with but a minimal involvement with any Union State activities other than his or her assigned class. *(Comes back toward seat and stands behind it.)* Now, I'm not saying Lydia Sweet will necessarily step into either of these scenarios. But I do say that we must take a hard look at her record at Union State thus far and attempt to extrapolate from it so that we can offer sound advise to the university administration. I realize money is by no means the primary issue here, but it certainly enters in.

(The lights on the conference room fade down as those on the D.L. area fade up. Lydia sits in one of two side-by-side chairs – suggesting part of a row in athletic field stands – watching the action on the field below. The actor playing Paul exits the conference room area and makes his way, sideways, across the row to the seat next to Lydia as Donald Sweet, Lydia's ex-husband. He hands her one of the two soft drinks he is carrying, and sits.)

LYDIA. Thanks, Donald.

DONALD. As I was saying...*(Looks down on field.)* Anything happen?

LYDIA. No. Still one out.

DONALD. Anyway, I realize money is by no means the primary issue here, but it certainly enters in.

LYDIA. *(Watching the game.)* How so?

DONALD. *(Watching the game.)* Well, if you eventually marry this guy, it will simplify my financial obligation somewhat.

LYDIA. Simplify being a euphemism for reduce.

DONALD. *(Good-naturedly.)* Right. I mean, I do have some mixed feelings. But regardless of my financial interest, overall I think it's great.

LYDIA. Y'know, Donald, I wasn't really planning on... *(Suddenly, Lydia jumps to her feet, yelling, as Donald applauds from his seat.)* Way to go, Terry.

DONALD. *(Proudly but quietly, to Lydia.)* Can that kid go to his left or can that kid go to his left? I still say he might have gotten an athletic scholarship even if you weren't a faculty member.

LYDIA. Well, he certainly plays shortstop better than he keeps secrets.

DONALD. No secrets from old Dad.

LYDIA. So I gather. He wasn't supposed to discuss this with anybody.

DONALD. My lips are sealed, Lydia.

LYDIA. Better than Terry's, I hope.

(Both applaud politely at something happening down on the field.)

DONALD. *(Looking at Lydia.)* So you think it's the real thing with this guy?

LYDIA. Aaron.

DONALD. Aaron.

LYDIA. I think so.

DONALD. That's wonderful.

LYDIA. *(Hooking her arm through his.)* You're a terrifically supportive ex-husband, Donald, as always. How do you stay so...detached? Don't you ever feel jealous?

DONALD. Sometimes. A little.

LYDIA. We really have remained friends. I'm grateful. And proud of us for that, y'know?

DONALD. So's Terry.

LYDIA. Yeah. He's up. *(Points to field.)*

DONALD. Hitless so far. He should bunt on this guy.

LYDIA. *(Cupping her hands around her mouth and yelling.)* C'mon, Terry. *(Wincing.)* Ooh.

DONALD. No way that's a strike.

LYDIA. *(Standing and yelling.)* Hang in there, Terry. Take him downtown.

(They both look to their left simultaneously, expressions of hopefulness quickly turning to disappointment. Lydia sits back down.)

28

LYDIA. Lucky catch.

DONALD. Oh for three today. There goes the average.

LYDIA. *(Looking at her watch.)* You think the game'll be over by six?

DONALD. I don't know. Maybe. You have to be somewhere?

LYDIA. I'm meeting Aaron.

DONALD. I figure Terry for one more at-bat. Don't worry about it. Go. Terry and I will have dinner.

(Donald watches the game. Lydia watches Donald.)

LYDIA. Y'know, Donald, I've always admired your levelheadedness.

DONALD. Not always.

LYDIA. It's helped sustain our friendship.

DONALD. Yeah. After helping kill our marriage.

LYDIA. Nothing killed our marriage, Donald. We just weren't meant to be...

DONALD. Lovers.

LYDIA. Spouses.

(Something on the field captures their attention. They both look to their left, and applaud. The lights on the D.L. area fade down as those on the D.R. area fade up. Aaron, informally dressed and wearing sunglasses, reclines on one of two side-by-side chaise lounges in a way that makes it difficult to determine whether he is napping, waiting, or observing. Lydia, also informally dressed, enters and starts to sit on the adjacent chaise lounge.)

AARON. *(Without moving a muscle.)* Not there.

LYDIA. *(Stops short.)* I thought you were sleeping. Why not?

AARON. It's broken. *(Pats the seat of his chaise and spreads his legs to make room.)* Sit here.

LYDIA. *(Looking around conspiratorially, but with an air of mischievous delight.)* I can't sit there.

AARON. Sure you can. It's easy. You just lean over backwards and surrender to the law of gravity.

(Aaron pats the seat again. Lydia starts to sit, stops, looks around, finally sits tentatively, perched on the edge of the chaise.)

AARON. *(Sarcastically.)* That looks comfortable. C'mon, Lydia, this is dangerous. You're gonna knock us both over.

LYDIA. It's safer this way, believe me.

AARON. Will you stop it? Lean back here. I've got room for you.

29

LYDIA. Better yet, we could just put a sign up. *(Stands.)* What is this, coming-out day?

AARON. No, it's the faculty picnic, bless its heart. Where everybody who's anybody lets down their guard.

LYDIA. *(Looking around.)* This isn't letting it down, Aaron, this is hurling it over a cliff.

AARON. For what? Sharing a chaise lounge? *(Leaning from side to side quickly so that the chaise shakes.)* Believe me, this thing couldn't handle us doing anything extra-curricular anyway.

LYDIA. No, but it's great at starting and confirming rumors.

AARON. How'd you get so paranoid? *(Pats the seat.)* C'mon.

(Giving in, Lydia sits down and leans back stiffly against Aaron.)

AARON. Relax. *(Pointing.)* The only ones who can see us are those two Foreign Language professors sitting under that oak tree—Is that an oak tree? I hardly know them anyway, and they probably speak broken English, so who are they gonna tell? What do you care if you're a hot Franco-Russian rumor? *(Hooks his arm around her waist.)*

LYDIA. *(Removing Aaron's arm.)* I saw Tom Grayson walking around a few minutes ago.

AARON. Tom Grayson teaches math, Lydia. He wouldn't notice if I started removing your appendix.

(Smiling, Lydia relaxes a bit.)

LYDIA. So, how are you enjoying the picnic, Dr. Kaplan?

AARON. It's picked up the last few minutes, Dr. Sweet.

(Aaron's hands disappear behind Lydia.)

LYDIA. Stop it, Aaron. If you even come near an erogenous zone, I'll be forced to report you to the Faculty Senate.

AARON. *(Sotto voce.)* I love you.

LYDIA. Not so loud.

(Aaron's arms encircle Lydia's waist, and he begins nuzzling her neck.)

LYDIA. Aaron, stop. I'm a nervous wreck.

AARON. *(Leaning back and raising his arms above his head.)* Okay, okay. Go. Sit in the other chair.

LYDIA. You said it was broken.

AARON. I lied.

LYDIA. I knew it.

AARON. You did not.

LYDIA. I did so.

AARON. Then why did you sit here?

LYDIA. Because I'm weak.

(She gets up, sits down in the adjacent chaise, and reclines.)

AARON. Look at this. We haven't even moved in together yet and, already, twin beds.

LYDIA. *(Looks over at him.)* I love you.

AARON.   Then live with me.

LYDIA. You're being self-destructive.

AARON.   No. Romantic.

LYDIA.   Same thing.

AARON.   I'll give you exactly ten seconds to remove your clothing and mount me.

LYDIA. *(Noticing something to the distant left.)* Oh, God.

AARON. Okay, I'll mount you.

LYDIA. Aaron.

AARON. What?

LYDIA. Here comes Tom Grayson.

(Both look to their left, wave, and offer wide, insincere smiles. The lights on the D.R. area fade down as those on the conference room fade up. It is the same meeting—well after dark. All are seated in their seats at the conference table. Silence all around.)

NED. *(Standing.)* Is that it then? Because if no one has anything further, we can proceed to the vote...votes. Clara. Anything?

CLARA. No.

NED. Marilyn? *(Marilyn shakes her head.)* Rick?

RICK. I'm ready.

NED. Paul, have I forgotten anything?

PAUL. Not that I know of.

NED. Fine. Then let's...

MARILYN. Ned. Wait. Excuse me.

NED. By all means. *(Ned sits.)*

MARILYN. Before we vote, I just want to... well, to vent a little, I guess. I'm not necessarily trying to sway any votes here, but since our interaction traditionally ends at this juncture, I figure this might be my last opportunity to

31

address the committee. *(The others express non-verbal impatience at yet another delay.)* In my group dynamics classes, it's usually my role as a facilitator to summarize and evaluate the group's process before we adjourn. So maybe that's what I'm doing now, I'm not sure. It's just that something continues to bother me about today's discussion. Part of it's personal, to be sure, but some of it relates to our behavior as a group. Anyway, I'd appreciate leaving here today with a bit more closure. So if I can beg your indulgence.

GEORGE. Okay, Marilyn, but keep in mind, I've got a sabbatical coming up in... *(Looks at his watch.)* ...eighteen months.

MARILYN. *(Smiling indulgently.)* Hang in there, George. This shouldn't take too long. I have to admit right off—and I say this knowing full well that I endorsed it at the time and was just as much a part of it as everyone else here—that it does bother me now that we broke precedent today by ignoring Ned's objections and discussing the two candidates together. I think we did so for a variety of reasons, including trust in one another's instincts and—let's face it—expediency. But I also think we were well aware of the kind of traps that lie underfoot in any undertaking of this nature, None of us are privy to the basic motivations or personal actions of most of our colleagues. Even when we know events to be true, we're never quite sure of their exact chronology. Why, at any moment, I would have difficulty describing, with any accuracy or in any detail, the life-styles or domestic arrangements of the vast majority of people in our department.

GEORGE. *(Leaning back.)* Thank God for that.

MARILYN. I agree, George. And yet here we are trying to predict the future behavior of candidates without having reliable handles on their past. Sometimes, it seems, we're barely able to pass judgement on their professional activities, let alone such nebulous areas as ethics or morality.

GEORGE. Hear, hear.

MARILYN. So what we're asked to do is use five or six years' worth of tenuous evidence to project the behavior of members of our Union State family over the next thirty years. Which we do, ignoring the fact that people change—some for better, others for worse—and ignoring the disheartening truth that what this exercise most resembles is a crapshoot.

NED. Forgive me, Marilyn, but at this hour I have to ask you to get to the point.

MARILYN. I apologize, Ned. I know I'm rambling. But I've never felt quite so frustrated by this whole process before. And this is the seventh or eighth tenure committee I've sat on. Somehow, the old democracy rationalization—you know, the worst system except for all the others—isn't helping me to feel we're doing any good here. Maybe we've opened up a can of worms today that's actually set us back several pegs.

NED. But what do we do, Marilyn? Abandon ship? Throw up our hands in dismay? You're not proposing we leave everything to chance?

MARILYN. No. But perhaps we have to confront our limitations and realize that it's a pretense to think that we can pass this kind of judgement. When I voted to delay the vote on Aaron, among my reasons was the fervent hope—and I'm sure I wasn't alone in this—that a useful additional insight or two would surface during the ensuing discussion. Well, I had an insight all right, but it was more distressing than useful. And it's been gnawing at me for the last hour or so. Why do I sense that we've been far more disapproving of Lydia than Aaron here today, despite what seems to be an approximately equivalent degree of respect for their professional achievements and performance? Have we perhaps encroached on an off-limits area that, rather than offering up truths about Aaron and Lydia, has merely served to expose our own inadequacies and prejudices—both as individuals and as a group? It scares me to admit it, but I have a strong fear that Lydia's future right now hinges on a decision that is being made by a committee guilty of a not-so-subtle form of sexism. Sexism. I was afraid to use the word before. I figured the reaction would be, 'here she goes again.' Consequently, in all this time, the issue never even came up.

RICK. Is this what you meant before by personal?

MARILYN. It's part of it. Because, believe me, I'm sure I'm guilty of this too, even as I'm taking offense. The other part of it is my own relationship with Lydia. Ned, should I stop? *(Several others nod "yes.")*

NED. No, go on.

MARILYN. When Lydia first started teaching here, I felt a certain degree of competitiveness with her, even though we taught different courses. We were, after all, two untenured women among the handful scattered throughout a faculty predominated by tenured men. I remember saying to her, early on, that however our relationship developed, we should probably try very hard to become and remain friends. I knew there'd be many a gathering where we would be virtually the only women in the room.

(The lights on the conference room fade down as those on the D.L. area slowly fade up. Lydia is sitting slumped down in one of a cluster of theater seats that suggests a row in a movie theater. The actress playing Marilyn exits the conference room and slips into the seat next to Lydia as Pat Hightower, Lydia's best friend. The lights up, Lydia begins writing in a notepad.)

PAT. *(Sitting up and looking around.)* Lydia, you're the only woman here.

LYDIA. *(Still writing.)* Except for you, Pat.

PAT. Don't any of the critics bring their wives?

LYDIA. *(Still writing.)* To a Monday morning screening of junk like this?

33

Hardly. I warned you about showing up early.

PAT. Oh, I didn't mind. It was fun. I've never been to a critics' screening before. Besides, I needed to talk to you.

LYDIA. So you said. *(Closes the notepad.)* Now what's this subject that's too hot for the telephone?

PAT. You want to go somewhere? Have lunch or something?

LYDIA . *(Glancing at her watch.)* Can't. I've got another screening at 11:30. We can talk here, can't we?

PAT. I guess.

LYDIA. What's the matter, Pat? You're starting to scare me.

PAT. Oh, it's nothing that severe. I enjoyed myself at your brunch yesterday.

LYDIA. *(Sarcastically.)* It must be quite a relief to have that off your chest.

PAT. No, I mean it. The food was great, and it was nice meeting some of your Union State friends.

LYDIA. I'm glad.

PAT. But I need to ask you something.

LYDIA. Ask away.

PAT. Are you, um... Are you having—or thinking of having—an affair with Aaron Kaplan?

LYDIA. What kind of question is that?

PAT. I'm not just being nosy, if that's what you think. It's just that I'm trying to avoid jeopardizing our friendship in any way or making a complete fool of myself. So tell me. *(Mock begging.)* Please. You don't have to tell me which—present, future, or unrequited fantasy. Just tell me whether to immediately back off or not.

LYDIA. I take it you like him.

PAT. Let's just say that, given a nudge, I could. Real easily.

LYDIA. And you're asking my permission?

PAT. No. Your intention. C'mon, Lydia, this is humiliating enough. Just tell me. What's the big deal?

LYDIA. Pat, this is crazy.

PAT. What's crazy? I know there's something going on between you two. I could tell by the way he reacted when I mentioned your name. I'm just trying to determine whether it's a playful, professional, platonic relationship—which I hope—or a soon-to-be or already-is sexual relationship—which I fear and which I am more and more sure of with every passing moment. You have three seconds to laugh hysterically and tell me I'm hallucinating. Time's up. Oh, well. Although the good ones come along once every Halley's comet, I hereby wash my hands of Aaron Kaplan. After all, you're my best friend, whereas he...is just a guy. *(Lydia, embarrassed, is looking down. Pat reaches out and turns Lydia's face so she can see it.)* He is just a guy, right, Lydia? Oh, my God, you're in love. *(Pat smiles.)* Why, you little devil, you. *(Lydia smiles embarrassedly.)* I've unearthed the big secret, huh? *(Disarmed, Lydia nods.)* My lips are sealed. *(Leaning toward Lydia.)* Tell me everything. *(The lights dim. Lydia points toward the screen, smiles at Pat and sits back in her seat. Pat then sits back in her seat resignedly.)* Shit.

(Lydia glances at Pat and smiles. The lights on the D.L. area fade down as those on the D.R. area fade up. Aaron, wearing only a bathrobe, lies on a bed, propped up against a pillow with his arms crossed behind his head. On a small table next to the bed is a telephone.)

AARON. *(Calling.)* You think they've finished yet?

LYDIA. *(Offstage.)* Who?

AARON. *(Calling.)* Who else? The committee.

LYDIA. (Offstage.) That depends. *(Lydia enters, drying her hair and wearing nothing but a bath towel.)* Open-and-shut endorsements fly right by, clear-cut negatives take a bit longer. But if there are all kinds of questions in people's minds, it can go on forever. They don't have to vote today, y'know. They could hold it over till the next meeting.

AARON. If they do, are we still going through with everything?

LYDIA. We said we would either way. Why? Are you getting cold feet?

AARON. No.

LYDIA . *(Sitting down on bed.)* I figure they approved you after fifteen minutes. The discussion on me will run through February.

AARON. Nah. That's your insecurity talking. You know it's just the opposite: they're having me for dinner and spitting out the pits. I'll bet the most common word used in that room today is 'lightweight.'

LYDIA. Don't be ridiculous. You're Mr. Union State. They'll call me an absentee employee, an egomaniac, a prostitute.

AARON. And don't forget your bad points.

LYDIA. Mine will be, I promise you, a crucifixion.

AARON. And you're not even Jewish. You think there's any chance of getting tenure if the department vote's negative?

(Lydia props herself up against the other pillow.)

LYDIA. Two. Slim and none. There's no way the University committee is gonna overturn the department vote.

AARON. And then what?

LYDIA. What do you mean?

AARON. Suppose we both get turned down.

LYDIA. We start job-hunting. Or found a small college in Antarctica.

AARON. And suppose one of us gets it and the other—namely, me— doesn't. What's our plan again?

LYDIA. I don't even want to think about that.

AARON. Okay. And speaking of no-win situations, where do we stand now if we both get it?

LYDIA. Who knows? We've been through these contingencies so many times, I can't remember what the hell we decided. I love you, Aaron, but I'm not sure turning my whole life upside down to force a happy ending makes any sense, you know?

AARON. Well, that's certainly reassuring.

LYDIA. C'mon, we're not teenagers.

AARON. I know, but we haven't exactly started spitting our teeth out either. You don't think we could live together—I mean really live together—and make it work?

LYDIA. I don't know. Neither of us has much of a track record at marriage.

AARON. Wrong jockeys in the saddle, that's all.

LYDIA. Maybe. Maybe not. To tell you the truth, the thought of going public bothers me. A lot.

AARON. You've just become habituated to being secretive, that's all.

LYDIA. No, it's more than that. I mean, even after we get tenure. If we do. I'm... embarrassed.

AARON. About what? Lying, you mean? Falling in love again? Or living in sin?

LYDIA. All of the above. I think I'm discovering that I'm hopelessly conventional.

AARON. To say nothing of conventionally hopeless.

LYDIA. You think we can be faithful to each other for the—gulp—rest of our lives?

AARON. Depends how long we live. I figure I'm not due for another intense relationship for about twenty-five years, by which time I will probably be dead and impotent, preferably in that order.

LYDIA. I prefer that order too. What time is it?

AARON. I have no idea. *(He lifts the telephone receiver to his ear, then replaces it.)*

LYDIA. What are you doing?

AARON. Making sure it's working.

LYDIA. Boy, you are nervous.

AARON. *(Looking around.)* Okay. What else can we do to pass the time till the phone rings? Canasta, anyone?

LYDIA. You really want to get married?

AARON. Not till I'm dressed.

LYDIA. I mean it..

AARON. I'm easy. Yeah.

LYDIA. How is it you're so sure about us?

AARON. Who's sure? I'm just in heat. I see it as the ultimate ménage a trois—you, me, and Union State.

(Playfully, Aaron rolls over onto Lydia.)

LYDIA. More tension to be relieved, I take it?

AARON. No, no. I just thought of a way to make the phone ring. We'll induce coitus interruptus.

LYDIA. It didn't work a half-hour ago.

AARON. Two's my lucky number.

(They kiss, embrace, and roll over. The lights on the D.R. area fade down as those on the conference room fade up. It is much later at the same meeting. All are slumped in their seats at the table, looking fatigued. Some are still filling out ballots, others are folding and passing them to Paul.)

GEORGE. I don't understand this idiotic precedent. What purpose does it serve to vote on tabling the vote by secret ballot?

NED. Just an extra level of insurance against peer pressure, George. I'm not thrilled about the prospect of postponing the vote. But I wouldn't want to rush this decision either. Are they all in, Paul?

PAUL. *(Counting the ballots.)* Six. Yeah.

NED. Okay. If the majority of them are abstentions, we adjourn and resume our discussion and vote a week from today. Unfortunately, that's the only time all of us are available to meet as a group again. But at least we'll have gained some measure of perspective, so we can stop going over familiar ground to no end. If the majority vote to vote, then that's what we'll do, immediately thereafter. Understood and agreed? *(Nods all around.)* Paul, count the abstentions.

PAUL. *(Opening the ballots, reading them out, and placing them in separate piles.)* Abstain... abstain ... abstain... vote... abstain... *(Stops.)* That's a majority already.

NED. Okay. Let's call it a day. Please, everybody, take your materials with you, so you can review them during the interim, and I'll see you next week, same time, same place.

GEORGE. *(Standing.)* Well, let's do this again...real soon.

(All but Ned gather up their belongings and rise.)

NED. Thanks very much, everybody. I know this has been difficult. And

37

I know no one's happy about having to meet again. Including the candidates. I'll call both of them tonight.

CLARA. *(As she stands.)* That'll only take one phone call.

GEORGE. Now, now, Clara.

RICK. *(To Ned.)* How much will you tell them?

NED. Only that we haven't voted yet.

MARILYN. Is anybody interested in going over to Kessler's for a drink? I know I could use one. Or is it too late?

RICK. I'm game.

PAUL. Sure. Why not?

GEORGE. *(Glancing at his watch.)* I guess I have time for... twelve or thirteen drinks.

NED. Why don't you head on over there? I'll catch up with you in a few minutes. I just have to make a few notes.

(All but Ned head for the exit.)

NED. Folks. One other thing. It's important that you—that we—refrain from discussing any of this outside this room. With each other, with the candidates, with anybody. I'm confident you'll abide by that. Thanks.

(Ned begins writing. Others exit.)

GEORGE. *(The last to go, before he exits.)* Ned. *(Ned looks up.)* Fat chance.

(The lights on the conference room fade down as those on the D.R. area fade up. Aaron and Lydia sit side-by-side in adjoining seats that suggest a two-seat row in an airplane. Lydia reads a magazine, Aaron a book.)

INTERCOM VOICE. *(Offstage.)* Ladies and gentlemen, this is Captain Fredericks again. Although the seat belt sign has once again been turned off, we recommend that you remain in your seats as much as possible for the remainder of our trip and keep your seat belts buckled. We should be landing at San Juan International Airport in approximately one hour and forty minutes. Thank you and enjoy the rest of your flight.

LYDIA. *(Looking out the window, which is on her side.)* Wanna see something?

AARON. Nope.

LYDIA. Almost forgot. *(Leaning toward him.)* We could've gone somewhere close, Aaron, so we didn't have to fly.

AARON. If you and the pilot will just refrain from reminding me where I

ACT TWO

(The conference room of Act One has been converted into a judge's chambers—via a modification of furnishings and props, including the addition of a desk—so that the resemblance between the two settings is striking. Jeff Kaplan pokes his head in the door.)

JEFF. *(Calling offstage.)* This way, Pop. Nobody here yet.

(Jeff holds the door open, letting Mort Kaplan enter, then follows him into the room. Both wear jacket and tie.)

MORT. *(Looking around.)* This is a judge's chambers? Big deal.

JEFF. Aaron said they could have used a courtroom downstairs, but they wanted to keep it small and simple.

MORT. So where are they?

JEFF. *(Glancing at his watch.)* They'll be here. We're very early, Pop.

MORT. That's okay. I like to be on time.

JEFF. *(Looking around the room.)* On time is when something starts. You like to be there the day before.

MORT. *(Sitting down.)* Who is this guy anyway?

JEFF. Ginsberg. Judge Joel Ginsberg.

MORT. The same one who did the divorce?

JEFF. Yep.

MORT. What is he, on retainer or something?

JEFF. *(Examining books in bookcase.)* He's the only judge either of them knew. So Aaron asked him.

MORT. And he works weekends?

JEFF. I guess so.

MORT. What's his fee?

JEFF. What is this, Pop, an oral exam? I don't know. And it's not a fee. It's

41

a donation.

MORT. Fee, donation. They could call it zucchini, it's the same thing. Jeff, c'mere. I want to ask you a question.

JEFF. *(As he walks toward Mort.)* For a change.

MORT. You think they'll have kids?

JEFF. I don't know, Pop. Lydia's son is a college kid already. *(Sits.)*

(Mort studies Jeff silently.)

MORT. So what's with you lately?

JEFF. No kids yet, Pop.

MORT. In general, I mean.

JEFF. Same as I said in the car. Fine. Really.

MORT. Think you'll ever marry?

JEFF. I was hoping Aaron's two marriages might count as one for each of us.

MORT. You know what I mean. When you're... you know...

JEFF. When I'm through this 'phase?' *(Jeff laughs.)* Y'never know, Pop. Y'never know.

(The lights on the judge's chambers fade down as those on the D.R. area fade up. Lydia, dressed casually, sits on a chair staring intently out toward the audience as if into a dressing mirror. Aaron enters, notices what she is doing, and squeezes into the same chair, directly behind her. He then moves his head forward until it is side-by-side with hers, facing the same direction.)

AARON. What are you looking for? Cracks in the mirror or pimples on your face?

LYDIA. Neither. I'm searching for signs of congenital insanity.

AARON. Uh oh. Second thoughts.

LYDIA. Second? They surfaced last week. These are eighth and ninth.

AARON. What's the matter?

LYDIA. Aaron, what are we doing?

AARON. We're getting married.

LYDIA. *(Conceding.)* Great.

AARON. ...We're buying a house ...

LYDIA. Fine.

AARON. ... And we're having a child.

LYDIA. *(Cringing.)* Oh, God.

AARON. Let's take this one step at a time, shall we? How about if we get dressed and go get married? We're due downtown in an hour.

42

LYDIA. *(Placing a hand on her belly.)* I'm not ready to tell anybody yet. Suppose I show.

AARON. At two months? *(Humoring her.)* I don't think so, Lydia.

LYDIA. My cheeks are puffy already. *(Points in the mirror.)* Look.

AARON. That's just a coating of depression and fear. You look adorable. *(He kisses her on the head and stands.)* Let's get ready.

LYDIA. *(Staring into mirror.)* I haven't been pregnant in nearly twenty years. I forget how.

AARON. It's easy. You just keep looking down until your feet disappear. C'mon.

LYDIA. Maternity clothes. Pain. Career interruption. Pain. Midnight feedings. Pain. No privacy. Pain.

AARON. Sounds great.

LYDIA. Why are we doing this? I forget. Remind me.

AARON. Because we love each other.

LYDIA. So what?

AARON. Because it would be unromantic to wait till the tenure ruling. This way, it's an unqualified commitment to each other. We've been through all this.

LYDIA. Keep going.

AARON. Because you remember almost nothing about the care of a small child and I never knew anything to begin with. Look at me. All I know how to do is teach teenagers how to write. The first time my child spits up, I'll probably grade it and return it to her. Do you realize you're being calmed down by a nervous wreck? I'm not very good at this.

LYDIA. That's becoming abundantly clear. What I'm trying to say, Aaron, is that this kid is forever.

AARON. Is that a plus or a minus?

LYDIA. Suppose we wake up a year from Tuesday and want out.

AARON. What do I look like, a Ouija board? I don't know. You lived through it once. So did Terry. And look how terrific he is.

LYDIA. That's true. But I'm still scared.

AARON. Who isn't?

LYDIA. Maybe we can find a way to give each other more security.

AARON. *(Removing his shirt and starting to exit.)* We're exchanging vows today. You wanna do consonants too?

(Exits.)

LYDIA. *(Calling.)* Promissory notes, maybe. 'I swear I will not dump you, no matter what. Signed, your spouse.' *(To herself.)* I think I'm too old for all this.

43

AARON. *(Offstage.)* Come get dressed, Lydia.

LYDIA. *(Still looking in the mirror, whining like a small child.)* I want tenure.

(The lights on the D.R. area fade down as those on the judge's chambers fade up. Jeff is standing at the bookcase, examining a book he has removed from it. Mort is sitting.)

MORT. Maybe you better put it back. He could come in any minute.

JEFF. I really don't think he'd mind, Pop. I wonder if he actually reads this stuff.

(Pat enters. Jeff replaces the book and approaches her. Mort stands.)

PAT. Hello. I'm Pat Hightower. I'm a friend of Lydia's.

JEFF. *(Shaking hands with her.)* Jeff Kaplan. I'm Aaron's brother. This is my dad, Mort Kaplan.

(Mort shakes Pat's hand.)

MORT. Nice to meet you. Nobody else seems to be here yet.

PAT. There are only two others coming. Lydia's son, Terry, and, uh, his dad. Donald. Terry stayed with him last night.

MORT. And where are Aaron and Lydia?

PAT. I spoke to Lydia about fifteen minutes ago. Sounds like they're running a little late. But she said the judge wasn't going to make it on time anyway. *(Terry enters, followed by Donald. To Terry.)* Hello.

(Pat approaches Terry and Donald, greeting each with a kiss.)

PAT. Terry, Donald, this is Jeff, Aaron's brother, and Aaron's dad.

(The four men shake hands all around.)

MORT. *(To Donald.)* You're...his father?

DONALD. Yes.

MORT. So you...were...

DONALD. Married to Lydia, yes. We're still good friends.

MORT. Sounds like.

JEFF. *(Spiriting Mort away.)* Let's grab some seats, Pop.

PAT. How's school, Terry?

TERRY. I'm on break now.

44

PAT. Oh, right.

MORT. *(Sitting down.)* So how does this thing work? Anybody know?

TERRY. The ceremony, you mean? *(Mort nods.)* I think the judge just says a few words, and then has them exchange vows, There's not much to it.

MORT. That's it? I'm at the hardware store longer than that. Donald, did you and Lydia have a big wedding?

DONALD. Yes. Fairly big, I guess.

MORT. Aaron did too. Boy, they sure make these things routine today. Maybe it's because it's their second one. I guess when marriages lasted longer, weddings did too. *(To Pat.)* Did you have a big wedding?

PAT. I had one very tiny one and one medium-size one.

MORT. You were married twice?

PAT. And divorced twice.

MORT. Oh. And how tiny was the tiny one?

PAT. We eloped.

JEFF. *(To divert him.)* Pop, what time do you have?

MORT. *(Holding his wrists up.)* No watch.

DONALD. *(Looking at his watch.)* I have ten of.

(Everyone is sitting by now. There is a long, tense, fidgety silence all around.)

JEFF. *(After a long pause.)* We really must do this more often.

(Everyone laughs and relaxes a bit. The lights on the judge's chambers fade down as those on the D.R. area fade up. Aaron and Lydia, handsomely but simply dressed, sit in adjacent seats as if in a car, with Aaron driving.)

AARON. Lydia, relax. I can hear your knees knocking.

LYDIA. I was fine until you nearly rammed into that bus.

AARON. I didn't nearly ram into it.

LYDIA. Call it what you want. All I know is I could count the treads on the right rear tire.

AARON. If you wanna drive, it's fine with me.

LYDIA. I couldn't. I'm too nervous.

AARON. Why? You talked to the judge. I thought he said he'd be at least fifteen minutes late.

LYDIA. He did.

AARON. *(Glancing at his watch.)* Well, we'll make it.

LYDIA. That's what I'm afraid of.

AARON. How do you think our families will get on?

LYDIA. Pat knows they haven't met. She'll introduce them. *(Looks out window.)* I suppose we should've gotten there before everyone so we could do that, but I figure we've got enough to handle for one day. *(Turns her head and looks behind them, then looks out window again.)*

AARON. Lydia, what are you looking for?

LYDIA. I'm hoping for a sign of some kind. Something to appear out of the blue and help me understand what the hell I'm doing. Like a dove landing on the roof of the car, or a roadblock that prevents us from getting there at all. A solar eclipse would do the trick.

AARON. How about the judge being late? You could use that.

LYDIA. Too inconclusive. Now if he had been kidnapped...

AARON. You want me to circle back and see if I can find that bus?

LYDIA. Don't bother. With my luck, you'll miss it again.

AARON. *(Laughing.)* You're an asshole, Lydia, but I love you. Tell me something. Do you really think I'm any more sure of any of this than you are? Well, I'm not. And if you promise not to take this as any kind of sign, I'll pull the car over and let you in on a little secret.

LYDIA. What?

AARON. Promise?

LYDIA. I promise.

(Aaron pulls the car over and stops.)

AARON. I've got to throw up.

(Aaron gets out of the car and exits. Lydia leans back and throws her hands over her face. The lights on the D.R. area fade down as those on the judge's chambers fade up. The same five characters are in the room, but they now sit more closely bunched, chatting convivially.)

DONALD. *(To Pat.)* Was that your first husband?

PAT. No, no. That was my second. Clark.

TERRY. The real estate guy?

PAT. Slum lord, y'mean. How he slept nights I'll never know.

MORT. *(To Jeff.)* Sounds like your cousin Mel. *(To others.)* I have a nephew who's a hotshot landlord. Only trouble is. Somewhere along the line he had his conscience removed.

JEFF. It was minor surgery, believe me.

TERRY. *(Jumping to his feet.)* I think they're here.

(Terry goes toward door. The others rise and follow him.)

PAT. Shouldn't we welcome them in some way?

MORT. Anybody got rice?

46

JEFF. That comes after, Pop.

PAT. How about just applause?

DONALD. Sounds good. *(He starts applauding.)*

(The door opens. Everyone applauds. Ronnie, certainly underdressed for the occasion but only slightly disheveled, enters. The applause stops abruptly.)

MORT. *(Startled.)* Ronnie! What are you...

RONNIE. Hello, Pop. Jeff.

JEFF. *(Tentatively.)* Hi.

MORT. *(Approaching Ronnie.)* It's nice to see you, Ronnie. How are you?

(Mort greets Ronnie with a kiss.)

RONNIE. I'm okay, Pop.

PAT. *(Extending her hand to Ronnie.)* I'm Pat Hightower. This is Donald Sweet. And Terry Sweet.

MORT. *(Starting toward chair.)* Ronnie. Come. Sit.

(Ronnie follows Mort. The others look at each other, confused. Mort and Ronnie sit.)

MORT. *(To Ronnie.)* You look good, you look good.

RONNIE. So do you. The last time...

JEFF. *(Approaching and interrupting her.)* Ronnie. *(She looks up.)* What's going on? *(No answer.)* I don't mean to be rude, but...why are you here?

RONNIE. I just thought I'd stop by for a bit.

JEFF. I don't get it.

RONNIE. I'm moving to California Tuesday.

MORT. That's great. Where?

RONNIE. Just south of L.A. *(To Jeff.)* Can't leave without saying good-bye.

JEFF. Ronnie, this is not a very good idea. I think you know that.

RONNIE. *(Settling back into her seat.)* Good or bad, it's what I'm doing.

PAT. *(To Jeff as she approaches him.)* Is there a problem?

JEFF. Could be. Ask her.

PAT. What's the trouble?

RONNIE. Trouble? Who said anything about trouble?

JEFF. C'mon, Ronnie. You can't do this.

RONNIE. Do what?

JEFF. Whatever it is you're doing. You can't just pop in and disrupt like this.

RONNIE. Oh, really?

PAT. If there's something you need to take up with Aaron and Lydia, I'm sure they'll listen. But this is the worst possible time.

RONNIE. Don't you think I know that?

(Jeff moves behind Ronnie's seat and pokes his head close to hers.)

RONNIE. If you're trying to smell my breath, Jeff, you're out of luck. I know it would provide a convenient explanation if I were sloshed, but I'm not. I had one or two drinks this morning, that's all.

JEFF. By your standards, that's stone-cold sober, huh?

RONNIE. Right now I'm as clear-headed as anybody here.

MORT. *(Sliding closer to Ronnie and patting her arm.)* Ronnie, Ronnie, Ronnie. Tell me what's got you upset. Maybe I can help. We could go someplace private where we could talk.

RONNIE. *(Stands.)* No, thanks. I'm staying right here.

TERRY. *(To Donald.)* Dad, why don't we wait outside?

DONALD. Sure.

(Terry and Donald start for door.)

RONNIE. Don't go on my account. What I have to say is for you too. You're Lydia's son, right?

TERRY. Uh huh.

RONNIE. And you're the ex?

DONALD. Yes. *(Points toward others.)* But this matter seems to be between you and...

RONNIE. No, no. Stay. Please.

(Donald looks at Pat as if for advice. Ronnie sits in a different seat, on the opposite side of the room from the door. Terry sits. Slowly, Donald sits.)

PAT. *(To Ronnie.)* I wish there was some way we could take care of this without...

RONNIE. There isn't.

PAT. It's not that no one wants to hear you out.

JEFF. Ronnie, could I talk to you out in the hall? *(Ronnie looks at Jeff but doesn't respond.)* Please?

RONNIE. I don't think so.

(Aaron and Lydia enter hurriedly.)

AARON. I know, I know. Late for our own wedding.

(Jeff and Pat rush toward Aaron and Lydia.)

JEFF. Aaron. *(Gestures across room toward Ronnie. Sotto voce.)* I think we've got a problem.

(Pat takes Lydia's arm.)

LYDIA. *(Turning back toward door.)* Oh, no.

RONNIE. *(Standing.)* Hello, Aaron. Congratulations.

AARON. *(Approaching Ronnie, and acknowledging Mort as he passes by him.)* Thank you. What's up, Ronnie? We don't have much time.

RONNIE. You're kidding. And I thought you two had the rest of your lives.

(Terry and Donald quietly approach, greet, and comfort Lydia.)

AARON. You know what I mean. Should we find another office?

RONNIE. For what? Don't tell me I'm out of place here.

AARON. Ronnie...

RONNIE. Lydia's ex-husband is here.

AARON. He was invited. And he's not out to embarrass anybody. Are you drunk?

RONNIE. *(Angrily.)* No, I'm not drunk. *(Sits.)*

MORT. *(Stands, walks toward the door.)* Why don't the rest of us wait outside?

RONNIE. No, don't. *(To Aaron.)* Tell them all to stay. I'll go in a few minutes.

AARON. *(To others.)* Wait a second. Everybody. Please sit down. *(To Ronnie.)* Why not go now? We can talk another time, can't we?

(Others take seats.)

RONNIE. I'm moving out of the area.

AARON. To a country without phones?

RONNIE. This won't take long.

AARON. Fine. *(Sits.)* What won't take long?

(The door opens. Judge Joel Ginsberg pokes his head in the room.)

JUDGE. Lydia? Aaron? Could I see you both in here please? Just for a moment. Thanks. *(Withdraws his head.)*

(Aaron and Lydia look at each other. Each stands, then looks around at the others. The lights on the Judge's chambers fade down as those on the D.L. area fade up. The Judge is removing his jacket so he can put on his judicial robe. Lydia enters, followed by Aaron.)

JUDGE. *(Turning to face them.)* Hello.

LYDIA. Hello.

AARON. Nice to see you again, Your Honor.

JUDGE. Can the Your Honor stuff, Aaron. You're not approaching the bench, you're marrying this lovely lady. That's your honor, not mine. *(Turns back and starts to put on his robe.)* I just wanted to talk to you for a minute about your guests today. I like knowing who the witnesses are so I can make a remark or two that makes them feel included. Tell me who they are—in general, I mean. How far they've come today, from where, how long you've known them, that sort of thing. Then we can decide just how much you'd like me to say today. *(His robe on, the Judge turns to face them.)* After all, it is your ceremony. If it were mine, I sure wouldn't want anyone deciding for me what... Did I read my calendar wrong? I thought I was due here today to marry you. You two look like you're on trial for crimes against the state. You can't be that nervous. *(No response.)* What's wrong? May I ask?

LYDIA. We have an uninvited guest, I'm afraid.

JUDGE. Oh? Who?

AARON. Ronnie.

JUDGE. *(Trying to place the name.)* Ronnie.

AARON. My ex-wife.

JUDGE. Oh, Ronnie.

AARON. Right.

LYDIA. And she's refusing to leave.

JUDGE. Is she in there with the others?

AARON. Yes.

JUDGE. And who are the others?

AARON. My father and my brother. A good friend of Lydia's. And Lydia's son and ex-husband.

JUDGE. *(To Lydia.)* Your ex too? *(Lydia nods.)* If I had known, I could have invited my ex-wife. We could have kicked off a trendy new sociological phenomenon. *(Lydia and Aaron laugh in spite of themselves. Placing a consoling hand on Lydia's shoulder.)* I'm sorry. I don't mean to be flip. I know this is a tribulation. *(Paces.)* If Ronnie merely wants to sit through the ceremony, you could, I suppose, grit your teeth and bear it, hoping that she does indeed hold her peace, if not forever, then at least for today. If she plans on heckling, however, or in any way obstructing the orderly procedure of the ceremony, I will of course have to take action. But this is all conjectural. *(To*

Aaron.) Would you like me to speak with her?

AARON. To tell you the truth, I'm not sure it would do much good. I don't mean any disrespect.

JUDGE. That's okay. Well, regardless, I don't want the two of you to worry about it. We will not allow her to ruin this day for you. *(Starts for the door.)* If she hasn't already.

AARON. Sir. *(Judge turns to face Aaron.)* What will you do?

JUDGE. Please understand. She cannot do this. I'll try to reason with her. But, if need be, I will simply have her removed from the room. Or the building.

AARON. I'd rather you wouldn't.

LYDIA. *(To Aaron, surprised.)* Why in the world not?

JUDGE. Let's hope it won't be necessary. I'll talk to her first, Aaron. And I will certainly try to minimize any further embarrassment to anyone.

AARON. I wish there was another way.

JUDGE. Sometimes there just isn't.

LYDIA. *(To Aaron, irritated.)* What do you propose we do?

AARON. I don't know.

LYDIA. I'm not sure I believe this. What are you worried about? Look what she's doing.

AARON. I know, I know.

JUDGE. No one's going to manhandle her. Just escort her outside.

AARON. You mean physically?

JUDGE. Aaron, mental removal is not very efficient.

LYDIA. Maybe Aaron doesn't want to get married today as much as he thinks he does.

AARON. No. That's not it at all. I love you, Lydia. I just...

JUDGE. Look, I don't want to do anything that's going to make matters worse. For either of you. So let's discuss this calmly and decide on a course of action. *(Beckoning.)* Come over here. *(Lydia and Aaron approach him.)* Okay, I feel calm. How about you, Lydia. Do you feel calm?

LYDIA. No.

JUDGE. Aaron?

AARON. No.

JEFF. Well, one out of three ain't bad. Now, let's explore our options here.

(The lights on the D.L. area fade down as those on the judge's chambers fade up. The six in attendance are all sitting, in somewhat of a semi-circle, with Mort and Ronnie to one side and the others clustered some distance away.)

JEFF. *(Responding to Ronnie.)* Maybe I would find it fascinating. Maybe all of us would. But I still think everyone—including you, Ronnie—would be a hell of a lot better off if you would just make yourself scarce before they come

51

back in here.

RONNIE. *(Stands.)* Now why would I come all this way just to beat a hasty retreat at the last minute?

PAT. To spare the innocent bystanders all this discomfort? How about that?

RONNIE. That is unfortunate. But it's also necessary. Maybe being close to Aaron or Lydia assures you a giant dose of discomfort at some point. I've certainly had mine. I guess everyone gets a turn sooner or later.

JEFF. *(Standing.)* But you can control that. You can leave.

RONNIE. I can. But I'm not. I wonder if Donald isn't the least bit curious to hear what I've got to say. *(Turning to Donald.)* How about it, Donald?

(Jeff sits.)

DONALD. I think you're being very rude and inconsiderate, if you want the truth.

RONNIE. The truth is rude and inconsiderate, Donald. Didn't you know that? *(Beat.)* Is that why you're here today, because you're so comfortable with the truth? Or is it because you're ignoring it?

PAT. Why don't you just leave him alone?

DONALD. *(To Pat.)* No, no, that's okay. *(To Ronnie.)* I don't know what you mean.

RONNIE. How did Lydia's relationship with Aaron start, Donald? When did it start? Do you know?

DONALD. I don't know or care. It's not my business.

RONNIE. Isn't it? You don't care about honesty from a... What is she now, a good friend, right?

DONALD. We're good friends, yes. That doesn't mean we know everything about each other's lives.

RONNIE. It's time to wake up, Donald.

JEFF. *(Jumping to his feet.)* Who the hell are you to be talking to him like this?

RONNIE. I'm the woman whose husband ran off with his wife. Who the hell are you to be talking to me like this?

JEFF. What is all this, Ronnie? You weren't happy with Aaron then. Since when do you want him back?

RONNIE. Who said I do? I just resent like hell the way this whole thing was handled. *(To Donald.)* Don't you?

DONALD. Lydia and I were already divorced.

RONNIE. Were you now? Well, I've got a news bulletin for you, Donald. This match made in heaven began not only before you were divorced but before you were even separated.

DONALD. That's not true.

52

RONNIE. Isn't it? Ask your son. *(To Terry.)* Is it true?

TERRY. *(After a beat.)* I don't know. Leave me out of this, please.

PAT. *(Placing herself between Terry and Ronnie.)* That's enough. Stop badgering everybody. There's something seriously wrong with you.

MORT. *(From his seat.)* Ronnie, please. Stop this.

RONNIE. *(Turning and approaching Mort.)* Remember how you consoled me during the separation, Pop? How difficult you said it must have been to have 'horses changed in mid-stream against my will'? That was rich. I thought about that one a long time.

JEFF. Where's all this self-pity supposed to lead? You're divorced. It's over. What good can any of this do?

RONNIE. I don't know. But I don't feel any worse than when I came in. In fact, I already feel a little better.

JEFF. Well, we're all happy for you. *(Gesturing toward off-stage.)* But this is coming at their expense.

PAT. To say nothing of ours.

RONNIE. This support is touching. *(Looking around at each person in the group.)* For a son, a brother, a friend, a mother, an ex-wife. *(Laughs sardonically.)* A pair of liars and cheats who've been defended to the death by their loved ones and rewarded by the courts. What a system.

JEFF. Welcome to the planet earth, Ronnie. And what are we supposed to do about all this? Assuming any of it's true anyway.

RONNIE. Oh, it's true, all right. I know how you're all looking at me, but I've got truth on my side.

PAT. Your version of it.

RONNIE. *(To Pat.)* I'll put 'my version of it' up against Aaron's, that's for sure.

JEFF. You already did. In court.

RONNIE. That was just two lawyers playing ping pong, and you know it. Aaron's the kind of person who forgets breakfast vows by lunchtime.

JEFF. As opposed to the paragon of virtue you so obviously are.

RONNIE. Look, I argued, I fought, I complained, I left. But I didn't lie, and I didn't cheat.

MORT. *(Standing.)* Neither did he, Ronnie. And I asked him, believe me.

RONNIE. *(Coming toward Mort.)* You think he'd tell you the truth about something like that?

MORT. Yes, I do.

RONNIE. That's just what you need to believe.

(Donald whispers something to Terry. They both stand and start for the door. Donald gestures to Pat that they are going outside. Ronnie notices.)

RONNIE. *(Loudly.)* I would just love to know when Lydia's separation from Donald became officially permanent.

TERRY. *(Wheels around.)* I don't see what any of this has to do with my parents.

RONNIE. *(Approaching Terry.)* I'll tell you what it has to do with them. If your mother had never met Aaron, your parents would still be together.

TERRY. I don't think so.

RONNIE. You go out in the hall and ask your dad when all chances of a reconciliation between them disappeared. You ask your mom when she met Aaron. Then you ask Aaron and Lydia to describe the timing of the two separations and two divorces. And pay particular attention to the number of times the three of them use the word 'coincidence' with a straight face.

DONALD. Are you suggesting a conspiracy of some sort aimed against you?

RONNIE. No. What I'm suggesting, Donald, is that Lydia left you because she met Aaron at Union State.

DONALD. Lydia and I separated. It was mutual.

RONNIE. *(Scornfully.)* Uh huh. Sure it was. You show me two people mutually splitting up, and I'll show you a liar and a fool. Each time I flirted with leaving Aaron, it was after a fight or some heavy disagreement. But when he left, I had no idea why. None. It was Lydia, pure and simple, no matter what he might have told himself or anybody else. Mine were threats, temper tantrums. I wasn't proud of them, but they sure didn't break any vows. His was the one-sided ending of a marriage.

DONALD. I'm sorry, but I still don't see what any of this has to do with me.

RONNIE. Check your calendar. Aaron and Lydia started working together months before she left... okay, months before you and she separated. You think there's no connection?

DONALD. Listen. This is none of your business, but we didn't just suddenly start having problems. Aaron or no Aaron, I'd say my marriage to Lydia would not have lasted.

RONNIE. Maybe not. But I can imagine the level of energy Lydia put into your marriage from the beginning of that semester onward. I know, because of the way Aaron was. No matter what you talked yourself into since, from that point on, you two didn't have a chance of making it work. And neither did we.

JEFF. *(From behind Ronnie.)* So?

RONNIE. *(Loudly, wheeling around.)* So. I want the truth. I don't know what divorce trials do, but they sure don't have much to do with truth. I want the record set straight. *(Turns back to Donald.)* And I can't imagine that you don't. Nobody's that blasé.

(Aaron, Lydia, and Judge Ginsberg enter.)

RONNIE. Well, well, the lucky couple. And Judge Ginsberg, dispenser of justice.

JUDGE. *(Approaching Ronnie.)* Hello again, Ronnie. *(Quietly.)* Could I speak to you in my other office, please?

RONNIE. What's wrong with right here? We're among friends and relatives. And ex-spouses.

JUDGE. *(Putting his arm around Ronnie's shoulder and walking her toward the far side of the room.)* Okay. Ronnie, my responsibility here today is to marry these two people in front of their invited guests. And my intention is to perform that task with as much efficiency and quiet dignity as I can muster. And what I need—what I must have—from you and everyone else here is a willingness to cooperate, so that we can get on with the ceremony. *(Judge stops in his tracks, as does Ronnie.)* Which means I must ask you to leave.

RONNIE. I'm not ready to leave.

JUDGE. I understand that. But ready or not. Ronnie, I'm asking that you be fair to the others here.

RONNIE. *(Stepping away from Judge and laughing derisively.)* Fair. That's a laugh, coming from you. Is that what you call what you were at my divorce trial? Fair?

JUDGE. Yes I do, Ronnie. I made my ruling honestly, based on the information presented to me, and without bias. That you weren't entirely happy with the outcome doesn't mean it was an unfair judgement. None of which has anything whatsoever to do with today. Today two people are being married. And I'm asking you again to leave my chambers so that we may proceed.

RONNIE. I want to ask Aaron and Lydia something.

JUDGE. Not now, Ronnie. No. The witnesses are already here.

RONNIE. Exactly. *(To Aaron and Lydia, as she approaches them.)* The trial's over, the judgement's in, the money and belongings are divvied up, and you two are getting married. Nothing to gain, nothing to lose. So you two tell me something in front of your witnesses...

JUDGE. *(Loudly.)* Ronnie. Listen to me. *(Ronnie stops, turns to face Judge.)* Try to understand. *(Judge approaches her.)* At the very least, you're disturbing the peace here. You are also in a courthouse. Which means that you are, if you continue to disrupt these proceedings, in contempt of court. There are court officers down the hall and police officers downstairs. Do you really want me to call them?

RONNIE. *(Staring intently at Judge before answering.)* Why haven't you already?

JUDGE. I was hoping it wouldn't be necessary.

RONNIE. *(Skeptical.)* Oh, yeah? Okay, call them. Boot me out of here. That would be nice and fair. *(Judge glances at Aaron. Ronnie notices.)* Aaron stopped you, didn't he? *(To Aaron.)* Why's that, Aaron? *(Approaches Aaron.)* Why did you stop him? *(No response from Aaron.)* Guilt?

(Aaron looks at Ronnie but doesn't answer. He then looks at Judge.)

JUDGE. Just say the word, Aaron.

LYDIA. *(Coaxing.)* Aaron.

AARON. *(Exasperated.)* Ronnie, what the hell do you want?

RONNIE. I want you to answer me honestly.

AARON. Answer what?

JUDGE. Aaron.

AARON. *(Approaching Judge.)* I know, Your Honor, I know. Can we just let her get this off her chest? Is that okay? It might be better all around.

JUDGE. If that's what you want.

LYDIA. It's not what I want

AARON. Darling, I'm sorry. *(Goes to Lydia.)* If it's too much, we'll have him call downstairs. I would just like to clear the damn air. Be done with it.

(Lydia looks at Aaron, then at Ronnie. She shakes her head in bewilderment, and walks over to Pat.)

JUDGE . *(Starting toward door.)* I'll be in the other room, Aaron. You can call me when you're ready to begin the ceremony. *(Stops and turns.)* By the way, I strongly recommend you decide in advance just how long this is to take.

RONNIE. I'd prefer that you stay, Your Honor. I think you owe me that.

JUDGE. I owe you no such thing.

RONNIE. Then I'd appreciate it very much if you would anyway. I promise it will only take a few minutes.

JUDGE. How few?

RONNIE. *(Glancing at her watch.)* I'll be out of here and you can start your ceremony...on the hour. How's that?

JUDGE. It's not my decision. Aaron.

AARON. Okay.

JUDGE. Lydia?

LYDIA. *(After a long pause.)* A nightmare with a time limit. *(Throws up her hands in dismay.)* Sure.

JUDGE. *(To Ronnie, as he sits.)* Get to it then.

RONNIE. *(Turning toward Aaron.)* That's exactly what I intend to do. *(To Aaron.)* I want you to tell me, now that everything's all over and your new life is beginning, just which came first. The end of our marriage or the beginning of your affair with Lydia?

LYDIA. *(Stands.)* Must you subject everybody to this? Can't the rest of us just leave and come back?

RONNIE. What are you afraid of, Lydia? You know what he's going to say. You've already heard it. But you being here... *(Looks around at the others.)* ...You all being here, is precisely the point. You all know Aaron. I just want you to watch him closely as he lies through his teeth.

AARON. This is pointless if you decide in advance that I'm lying.

RONNIE. Pointless? No. At least I know that everyone here will see—and finally know—just what kind of person you are.

AARON. Ronnie, my marriage to you ended before my 'affair,' as you put it, began. Is that good enough?

RONNIE. You left out 'to all intents and purposes.' *(To Jeff.)* Do you believe him?

JEFF. What's the difference? Right now, even if Aaron's nose started growing, I wouldn't give you the satisfaction of noticing.

RONNIE. How about you, Pop? *(Points to Aaron.)* Look at his face. If anybody knows he's lying, you do.

(Mort looks at Aaron, then back at Ronnie, but says nothing.)

PAT. It's none of my business, but this is simply a jilted lover's obsession, nothing more, nothing less.

RONNIE. You're right. It is none of your business.

AARON. Ronnie, you're trying to get at the precise moment when my allegiance switched. I can't possibly know when that was. Who the hell can pinpoint the moment when love begins? Or ends. You can ask me a million questions or you can ask me the same question a million times. But the same thing's gonna keep coming up.

RONNIE. Right. Lies.

AARON. No. Not lies. Truths that you can't swallow. And they're never gonna satisfy you. Never.

RONNIE. But you did cheat on me.

AARON. I did not.

RONNIE. And you lied to me. As well as to everyone else here.

AARON. True. Lydia and I decided to keep our relationship a secret during the tenure rulings. But it was a deception aimed at the university. Only Terry knew.

LYDIA. Donald too.

RONNIE. Did he? *(To Donald.)* Tell me, Donald, when you found out that Lydia was involved with Aaron, didn't it seem kind of sudden? Did you think it just evolved overnight into a serious relationship?

AARON. *(Intervening.)* If you're asking whether I knew Lydia when you

57

and I were still married, the answer is yes. If you're asking whether I liked Lydia when you and I were still married, the answer is yes. If you're asking whether I was friends with Lydia while you and I were still married, the answer is yes. If you're asking whether I was attracted to Lydia while you and I were still married, the answer is yes. But if you're asking whether I slept with Lydia while you and I were still married, the answer is no.

RONNIE. *(Comes up close to Aaron.)* No, that's not what I'm asking at all. That would be a waste of time because your answers are so predictable. For all I know, they might even be true. What I want to know is—the question that really matters is—whether you knew you were eventually going to sleep with Lydia while you and I were still married. Answer me that.

AARON. That's a preposterous question. It's impossible to answer.

RONNIE. Bullshit. *(Turns and moves in the other direction.)* No-fault divorce was invented to protect people like you. Right, Judge?

(Judge does not respond at all.)

AARON. Who are people like me?

RONNIE. People who have to invent excuses to justify their behaviors. You wanted out, so you told yourself we were hopelessly incompatible. But you didn't have the courage to just go and admit that you had found somebody else, and then take your lumps. Not you. You had to make me the villain so your leaving was seen as the solution to a problem instead of the start of one. You even embarrassed me in print, you sarcastic son of a bitch.

AARON. *(Quietly.)* That was a stirring speech, Ronnie, but you're a little mixed up. Our problems preceded Lydia by years. You've conveniently altered the chronology of everything to make your case. I don't know if you've done it consciously, but you've done it.

RONNIE. If you had your way, I'd be like Donald here, talking myself into believing that we merely drifted apart to our mutual benefit.

LYDIA. Donald said that because it's true.

RONNIE. You may say that here, and Donald may say that here, but you both know in your hearts that that explanation is nothing more than an anesthetic for the pain. Or is it the ego? We'll just have to wait for Donald to wake up one morning and realize he's been had.

LYDIA. *(Angrily.)* Hey.

DONALD. I wish everybody would stop protecting me. This is actually quite interesting in a grotesque sort of way.

RONNIE. *(To Donald.)* Well, I'm glad you're being entertained. You sure are good at locking the truth out on the porch.

DONALD. The only truth that has absolutely revealed itself to me today has been the rather dispiriting fact that Terry is about to begin living in a house with a man who used to be married to a dipshit.

RONNIE. That's the ticket, Donald, a sliver of anger. Keep it up, you might get somewhere.

LYDIA. *(To Ronnie.)* You ought to be ashamed of yourself.

RONNIE. Horsewhipping would be too good for me, huh, Lydia? My, my, we must have struck a nerve.

LYDIA. All you've done is display your own lack of sophistication.

RONNIE. *(Goading, moving a step toward Lydia.)* Tell me more.

LYDIA. You're trying to construct some kind of simplistic, black-and-white explanation for something very complex. Every marriage has problems, and every married person has ambivalence. Once a marriage ends, of course you can create a case for premeditated disaffection. It's always there. So pointing it out after the fact proves absolutely nothing. A six-year-old could see that.

RONNIE. *(Moving closer to Lydia.)* I wonder if that same six-year-old could see that you're pregnant.

(Taken aback, Lydia reels a bit. All heads turn in her direction. She does nothing to deny it.)

RONNIE. This couldn't have anything to do with you two getting married, could it? *(Turns to Aaron.)* Aaron Kaplan having a baby. Could this be unqualified love at last? Or just an alternative to abortion?

MORT. *(Angrily.)* Stop this.

RONNIE. Stop what, Pop? If you're offended by the very mention of abortion, imagine how you'd feel if you went through one just because your husband wasn't ready for children?

AARON. Ronnie, you'll never change. *(Disgustedly, sits.)* I was ready for children. What I wasn't ready for was a lifelong commitment to a marriage that didn't work. No way I'm subjecting a child to that. Or to the odds on you not drinking for nine months. And if you want to parade around like somebody whose principles don't allow for the concept of abortion, go right ahead. But you and I both know better.

RONNIE. All I know is that I figured if our marriage didn't last, at least I'd come out of it a mother. I certainly expected I'd have a child by now. And I still can't figure out why I don't.

AARON. You don't because you weren't married to someone who could blot out problems at home the way you could.

RONNIE. *(Turning toward Lydia.)* No blotting out with good old Lydia, though, huh, Aaron? A goody-two-shoes Mommy turns up at last.

JEFF. Well, that about wraps up the Miss Congeniality competition. Ronnie by a landslide.

TERRY. *(Going to Lydia.)* Mom? You really are? *(Smiling weakly, Lydia nods.)* Well, that's great. *(Hugs her.)*

AARON. I was wrong, Ronnie. I should have just let them kick you out of here. It's amazing how wrong you are about everything.

RONNIE. *(Looking at Lydia.)* Obviously not everything.

LYDIA. *(To Ronnie.)* How could you possibly have known?

RONNIE. I didn't. Congratulations. If you're lucky, Aaron will let you go through with it.

MORT. *(Stands.)* Ronnie, I want you to go now.

RONNIE. In a few minutes, Pop. I've still got...

MORT. *(Walking toward door.)* I don't care. I want no more of this. *(Arrives at door. Announces to everyone.)* Either this stops or I go.

(Ronnie looks at Aaron, who says nothing.)

MORT. I wish you the best of luck in California. I'll see you out.

(Ronnie looks around, hesitates a moment, then exits, followed by Mort.)

PAT. *(Going to Lydia.)* Are you okay?

LYDIA. I'll survive.

AARON. *(Throwing up hands.)* I am sorry.

LYDIA. Part of me wants to send you off with her, you know.

AARON. I know. *(Smiles.)* But no part of me wants to go. I love you.

(Aaron and Lydia embrace. Judge stands, Mort enters.)

DONALD. Has she gone?

MORT. Yes.

JEFF. Who was that masked woman? I didn't even get a chance to thank her.

MORT. It's not funny, Jeff. She's very confused and angry.

PAT. That's no excuse, though.

MORT. I'm not excusing her. I'm just saying that ... *(To Lydia.)* Forgive me, but what she did today took a lot of chutzpah. Courage.

LYDIA. I know.

MORT. But even more insensitivity. I want to offer you my congratulations too. *(Hugs Lydia.)*

LYDIA. Thanks... Pop.

MORT. *(Turning to Aaron.)* You kids don't do things in exactly the order I had in mind. But...who's complaining? *(Hugs Aaron.)*

JUDGE. Remember me?

(All turn to face Judge.)

AARON. Before we start, can I just apologize to everybody? I'm really sorry about all this.

PAT. That's not necessary. Everyone here understands.

LYDIA. No. I want to apologize too. Not just for putting you through all this, but for holding out on everyone for so long. Aaron and I have gotten much too used to keeping everything to ourselves. Well, no more. I want you all to know that you're very much a part of the very privacy I'm always trying so hard to protect. And that's exactly why we wanted you here today.

JEFF. And warmed us up with such a lavish and memorable floor show.

AARON. Your Honor, I believe we're finally ready.

JUDGE. *(Moving downstage-left.)* Why don't we gather over here? *(Judge faces audience and indicates the area directly in front of him. Aaron and Lydia move directly in front of him and face him. The lights fade down everywhere but on the small area in which Judge, Aaron, and Lydia stand. The other six actors move stage-right and gather in a small circle as the faculty members they originally portrayed.)* I hope Aaron and Lydia won't mind too much if I add my personal voice to the select chorus chosen—who knows by whom?—to usher in their wedding day.

(The lights fade down on the Judge, Aaron, and Lydia, and fade up on the group of six faculty members.)

NED. Where are we. Paul?

PAUL. *(Counting the ballots in one of the two stacks in front of him.)* Still a few to go on Lydia.

(The others pass their ballots to Paul.)

PAUL. That's six. We're ready.

NED. Okay. Read them out.

PAUL. *(Opening the ballots, reading the votes, and placing them in two piles.)* Aaron first. Yes...yes...no...yes...yes...yes. Five yes, one no for Aaron Kaplan. *(Reaches for other stack.)* Lydia Sweet. Yes...no...yes...no...yes...yes. Four yes, two no for Lydia Sweet. Majority recommendations for both.

(The lights fade down on the faculty members and fade up on Judge, Aaron, and Lydia, still standing as before.)

JUDGE. *(To Aaron and Lydia.)* If you will, an afterword to the scene I just witnessed as well as a foreword to your ceremony. Two birds with one measly stone. *(To everyone.)* The note of solemnity that's been sounded on this otherwise joyous occasion seems to me a reminder of the formidable task confronting those of us who still embrace matrimony—in the sense of trying, trying again when at first we don't succeed: and I include myself in this august and romantic body—as well as those of us who have to pass judgements on confrontations between recently sundered conjugal partners. We live in an age characterized by long life, where a nuptial pledge of everlasting devotion makes a Supreme Court appointment seem short-lived by comparison. These inebriated pledges, however well-intentioned and heartfelt, are merely eloquent nuggets of wishful thinking. And sometimes—more often than not, it seems—they do not stand the severe test of time. So we judge those around us, even our loved ones, harshly. We jump to conclusions, we weigh what scant evidence we can produce, we perceive in all our splendid subjectivity. And we bemoan the perilous state of contemporary marriage. An adjustment is surely in order. Just what that should be—whether the nature of the pledges, the handling of divorces, or the very definition of marriage itself—we are not yet sure. We do know that a marriage meant to last forever is our most civilized and educated guess at an answer. Our problem is...we don't know the question. *(Raises his arms as if inviting everyone present to step in closer.)* Shall we get married?

(Slowly, the lights fade as... Curtain.)

ATTACK OF THE MUSHROOM PEOPLE

ISBN 0-88734-308-2

A humorous, thought provoking comedy-drama by Gary L. Blackwood. Winner of the Ozark Writers Conference. Cast of two (1m, 1f). Simple interior set.

No, the mushroom people are not the ones from that Japanese science fiction movie. Harry Frisbee is an aspiring but rejected poet who kidnaps a very drunk editor, Dina Vandegriff, in order to get his poetry read. In the ensuing days and nights a poignant battle of the sexes, wits and wills evolve. The characters are sensitive and carefully defined and their conflict is all too realistic. Do you do what you want with your life or do you sacrifice for security? ---- In this drama is food for thought. Margaret Menamin of the **Daily News** *said* "...I think Blackwood might as well get down to brass tacks and admit he's written a first rate thumbs up comedy."

NEARLY DEPARTED

ISBN 0-88734-212-4

An intriguing farce by Vincent D. O'Connor. Cast of eight (4m, 4f). Single set.

Alan, who has two mistresses intent on marriage, decides that his wife, Joan, no longer loves him and so he wants to end their relationship, but without a divorce. He arranges for an accident in which he "dies" and only ashes are supposedly left. All goes as planned until Alan discovers that his distraught "widow" is carrying the ashes in the jewelry box whose false bottom contains the necessary papers for his new identity. In order to retrieve the papers Alan enlists the reluctant aid of his brother-in-law, in whose house both the wake and funeral are being held. Close call after close call ensues, when the "dead man" must finally hide in his own coffin to keep from being caught by his wife and mistresses.

OH, MR. PRESIDENT

ISBN 0-88734-206-X

A sensually funny comedy by Bill Majeski. Cast of twelve (7m, 5f). Two simple interiors.

The President of the United States is scheduled to head a critically important international peace conference, but he is suffering from emotional and physical exhaustion. The Secretary of State has a solution...the President must be cloned. Professor Kenesaw, an eccentric but recognized genius, creates a virile duplicate. The new president, his mind banks strained by the hasty construction, is unpredictable. One obvious problem is the clone's romantic alliance with the professor's shapely assistant.
The real President, secretly carted away for a rest, returns undetected and there are two presidents in the White House. The complications continually create riotously funny misunderstandings and to everyone's surprise the conference is an astounding success.

See current catalogue for prices.